# God Has Your B.A.Q.

## (Biblically Answered Questions)

*Mark Hamric*

WestBow
PRESS
A DIVISION OF THOMAS NELSON

WestBow Press books may be ordered through booksellers or by contacting:

WestBow Press
A Division of Thomas Nelson
1663 Liberty Drive
Bloomington, IN 47403
www.westbowpress.com
1 (866) 928-1240

Because of the dynamic nature of the Internet, any web addresses or
links contained in this book may have changed since publication and
may no longer be valid. The views expressed in this work are solely those
of the author and do not necessarily reflect the views of the publisher,
and the publisher hereby disclaims any responsibility for them.

Any people depicted in stock imagery provided by Thinkstock are models,
and such images are being used for illustrative purposes only.
Certain stock imagery © Thinkstock.

ISBN: 978-1-4908-1599-2 (sc)
ISBN: 978-1-4908-1601-2 (hc)
ISBN: 978-1-4908-1600-5 (e)

Library of Congress Control Number: 2013921098

Printed in the United States of America.

WestBow Press rev. date: 12/27/2013

God Has your B.A.Q. Biblically Answered Questions
Written by Mark A. Hamric
Illustrated by Deanna Long
September 3, 2013

*Abstract:*
This work is written in a questions and answer format that attempts to answer the many varied question people typically ask Christians about their beliefs. These questions came from real people from all over the world. The answers I give come from my own personal studies and life experiences. I do not clam to be a trained Apologist or Theologian. Because the questions were spread out over a period of time and from different people some of them will have very similar themes and answers, however I did treat each question independently.

# Acknowledgements

*"Tread softly, for you are walking on the tears of those who walked before you."* Reinhardt Bonnke

I wish to thank all of those who believed in me while I was writing and assembling this book. Mira Banks, my prayer partner and warrior in the spirit. Pastor Beechard Moorefield, my mentor for over twenty years. Deanna Long, whose art is on the cover and the maps she sketched. Most of all I wish to thank all those inquisitors whose questions sent me on a journey for answers. I pray that I answered you well and that you were at the very least inspired to seek the truth beyond the material world.

Quotes came from, www.ochristian.com

# Author's Biography
# (a letter to the reader)

Beloved,

I dub you Thē ozē teō, which means "one who seeks the Mysteries of God." I am neither scholar nor trained apologist but I am a thē ozē teō in that I am one who will search out the scriptures and seek what God has revealed to us through them. Although I have not read much of other men's thoughts in any of these matters, I think they have influenced me. Ever since the outpouring of the Holy Spirit, He has testified of the glorious Gospel, by which men have done many good deeds of faith that has benefited all of humanity for nearly 2000 years. So that no one can say, 'I stand alone' in any knowledge of truth. I write therefore by these influences and from my own studies of both secular and faithful writers and as we all know, from those influences that seek to pollute the truth. We must always rely upon the Holy Spirit for guidance towards that truth.

Having not been raised by religious parents and being a very shy child whose schooling was rather mundane my fondest memories of childhood were of the stories from the Bible when teachers were still permitted to do so. I think if not for these teachers and the prayers of certain Godly people, many of whom have gone home to be with the Lord, my life would have been much darker than it was. My purpose now is to give back a work that with God's blessing will not only be attributed to me but to those wonderful praying people whose faith I shall never match and yet with the wisdom which God has shared these answers that they will touch so many of you thē ozē teō ens.

I do not claim to be righteous by anything I have done and certainly not more virtuous than most people, I give God thanks for all He has accomplished in me. Having stumbled through life with many ups and downs which is equally mundane as my schooling I have this bright spot that as a young man and a father at the time I finally stumbled to a place where when I cried to God he found me and from there He taught me. First much like a disciple I spent all my free time getting to know Him and asking questions, more and more questions, and He fed me the answers well chewed and sweet as milk right out of the Bible till I could begin to share them with others.

Sadly, I soon found out that no one cared. The people I thought to be my friends avoided me, some called me crazy and fanatical; Christians called me a heretic. The world outside of Christ was not ready and those who called themselves Christians were not ready. So, the Lord showed me a place where I could go and grow, at the time it was called New Life Family Worship Center A.G., in Winston Salem, NC led by Pastor Beechard Moorefield. After a month of regular attendance, Pastor Moorefield confirmed most of the things the Lord had taught me during that time of solace and what I think of as a consecration period. I attended there for many years and brought up my children there. It is now Called New Life International Pentecostal Fellowship; under this new name, we support ministries in many foreign countries. Although I am not always present, I still call this my home church and have the greatest respect for pastor Moorefield, and pastor Elect Brian Gaither. Without pastor Moorefield's strength and steadfastness, I might have significantly erred in my understanding of scripture. So to God be the glory of this rendering of knowledge from these most Godly influences which I am blessed to have been a part of and now impart to you beloved Theōzēteō.

Sincerely,
Mark A. Hamric

# Preface

Have you ever wondered about some of the things Christians believe? Alternatively, if you are a Christian, then have nonbelievers, atheist, and perhaps seekers ever asked you about things that you could not answer?

I have compiled several of these questions and prayerfully sought the answers. This book is the results of my endeavor. I have kept the questions exactly as asked online except for grammatical corrections along with any comments or purpose the inquisitor included. My answers to these varied peoples come from many years of meditation and study of God's word and my own personal walk with the lord. I use scriptures from the Authorized King James Bible (KJV) unless indicated otherwise.

I am 'old school' and prefer the A.D. *(Anno Domini)* and B.C. *(Before Christ)* dating systems where questions refer to some historical event I use these in lieu of the politically correct C.E. *(Common Era)* and

B.C.E. *(Before Common Era)* except when they are part of the original question.

Some questions are opinion based and have neither historical nor theological answers, in such cases the answers are my opinion and are not biblical apologetics. Other questions may contain assumptions and I am merely dispelling the assumption about mainstream Christianity and giving the enquirer a more rounded concept of the issue.

My hope is to give a well thought out response to the many and varied questions that many Christians are asked and in the process help many Christians to rethink some of popular but perhaps false teachings that have permeated the churches.

~~~

# Table of Contents

*"The Word of God well understood and religiously obeyed is the shortest route to spiritual perfection. And we must not select a few favorite passages to the exclusion of others. Nothing less than a whole Bible can make a whole Christian." A.W. Tozer*

*"An honest man with an open Bible and a pad and pencil is sure to find out what is wrong with him very quickly." A.W. Tozer*

# Chapter 1

# Studying and Comprehending the Bible

*"They are not the best students who are most dependent on books. What can be got out of them is at best only material; a man must build his house for himself." George Macdonald*

1. Do you have to read the Bible and go to Church to be a Christian?
2. Which English language Bible translation is most true to the Hebrew Old Testament text and Greek New Testament text respectively?
3. How is it possible that a god could cause The Bible, to be written containing "God's words," but fail to make it so clear that the littlest child and the dumbest heathen would instantly understand precisely what the god wanted them to know?
4. Can the Bible be interpreted anyway you want?
5. What is the best text or video summary of the New Testament?
6. What should everyone know about the Bible?
7. If God exist why hasn't he ever talked to me?
8. How do we know that The Bible wasn't tampered with by people in power who wanted to use the texts to their advantage?

**Q.** Do you have to read the Bible and go to Church to be a Christian?

I believe that God is actually there, but I'm wondering that if you are a Christian, do you have to read the Bible every day, go to church, and other stuff Christians do. I want to be one, and every Christian friend I have say that it's easy, but I don't know… For me it sounds hard!!

**A.** Being a disciple of Jesus is not easy and it's something you have to want. Being a Christian is very easy. If you want to get "Born Again," then all you need to do is ask Jesus to save you. But, unless you want to have no real understanding of who Jesus is then you need to read a Bible. You should begin to pray to God in the name of Jesus and ask Him to teach you about life and what your role in life is.

Jesus said, "So I tell you, don't worry about the things you need to live—what you will eat, drink, or wear. Life is more important than food, and the body is more important than what you put on it" (Mathew 6:25 ERV). What do you think He meant by that?

I think Jesus is saying that He made you to be someone wonderful and He wants to show you all that you can be but if you are too busy with getting food and clothes and worrying about how good you look, then you will miss the important things He wants to teach you.

There are many churches and if you desire to know who God is I would recommend first reading His word, and then asking Him to lead you to a good church where you can grow in your understanding of Him. The most important thing is to open up the communication by asking Jesus to come into your heart, and showing you His truth. He will do nothing without your permission. The greatest words of Jesus to the world in the Bible are, "look, I stand at your door and knock, if you hear me and open the door to me I will come in and dine with you and you with me" (Revelations 3:20). It is an offer of friendship and I will tell you a little secret, Jesus brings food for life.

~~~

**Q.** Which English language Bible translation is most true to the Hebrew Old Testament text and Greek New Testament text respectively?

The choice of words to represent in modern language what was expressed over 2000 years ago in the Old and New Testaments is a topic for broad debate - however I am seeking opinions on the most accurate translations of both.

**A.** It is probably less important to get an accurate translation, than one that you can actually understand. Still it is important to get one as accurate as possible and so my personal choice is the King James Authorized Version from 1769. It is by far the most popular version readily available. It is also the only version for which you can get a complete and exhaustive concordance.

If you are not sure what an "Exhaustive Concordance" is then allow me to explain. A concordance is a list of words from the Bible with every chapter and verse they are found in. This can be very useful when studying scriptures when you want to compare words and how they were used in different verses. Many Bibles have a small concordance in the back. An exhaustive concordance has every word in the Bible is listed and where it is found. Some Concordances go a step further and provide lexicons *(dictionaries)* that explain the words roots and show the various ways it may have been translated to English. Let me show you how to do a typical word study. I chose the word <u>Comforter</u> for this example.

The main Concordance will show you every occurrence of the word you are studying.

> Ecclesiastes 4:1 So I returned, and considered all the oppressions that are done under the sun: and behold the tears of *such as were* oppressed, and they had no comforter[H5162]; and on the side of their oppressors *there was* power; but they had no comforter[H5162].

> Lamentations 1:9 Her filthiness *is* in her skirts; she remembereth not her last end; therefore she came down wonderfully: she had no comforter[H5162]. O LORD, behold my affliction: for the enemy hath magnified *himself.*

> Lamentations 1:16 For these *things* I weep; mine eye, mine eye runneth down with water, because the comforter[H5162] that should relieve my soul is far from me: my children are desolate, because the enemy prevailed.

> John 14:16 And I will pray the Father, and he shall give you another Comforter[G3875], that he may abide with you for ever;

> John 14:26 But the Comforter[G3875], *which is* the Holy Ghost, whom the Father will send in my name, he shall teach you all things, and bring all things to your remembrance, whatsoever I have said unto you.

> John 15:26 But when the Comforter[G3875] is come, whom I will send unto you from the Father, *even* the Spirit of truth, which proceedeth from the Father, he shall testify of me:

John 16:7 Nevertheless I tell you the truth; It is expedient for you that I go away: for if I go not away, the Comforter G3875 will not come unto you; but if I depart, I will send him unto you.

The Table below I created to break down the Lexicon use in the back of the Concordance.

| What is in the Concordance | What it means to You |
|---|---|
| G3875 | This is the number with every interpretation of paraklētos. The "G" associates the word as Greek. |
| παράκλητος | Original Greek writing. |
| paraklētos | The Greek word written in English. |
| par-ak'-lay-tos | Pronunciation |
| An *intercessor, consoler:* - | An English definition of paraklētos |
| advocate, comforter | A list of all the words translated from paraklētos, G3875 in the KJV. |
| H5162 | This is the number with every interpretation of nâcham. The "H" associates the word as Hebrew. |
| נחם | Original Hebrew writing. |
| nâcham | The Hebrew word written in English. |
| *naw-kham'* | Pronunciation |
| A primitive root; properly to *sigh*, that is, *breathe* strongly; by implication to *be sorry*, that is, (in a favorable sense) to *pity, console* or (reflexively) *rue*; or (unfavorably) to *avenge* (oneself): - | An English definition of nâcham. |
| comfort (self), ease [one's self], repent (-er, -ing, self) | A list of all the words translated from nâcham, H5162 in the KJV. |

The letter "G" in the number denotes it was from the Greek, an "H" would be from a Hebrew word. If you then look up all the words associated with the numbers and how they were used in Scripture, you go a step beyond a mere definition into a deeper word study.

~~~

**Q.** How is it possible that a god could cause The Bible, to be written containing "God's words," but fail to make it so clear that the littlest child and the dumbest heathen would instantly understand precisely what the god wanted them to know?

**A.** Could God have caused the Bible to be written so that everyone could understand it? Perhaps He could have, but why He did not is because inside the heart we know right from wrong. Our free will is of a great value to God and a great Gift from God. We have all misused this amazing gift and yet God still tolerates us awaiting the time when we make the only righteous choice available which is to turn from our way to His. God's ways are not our ways; in His sovereignty, He chooses His own way of bringing each of us, who will trust Him, to the knowledge of the Truth. In other words, God wants to meet with us individually and guide us daily. The Bible is His tool but without faith in Him, no one can understand it.

In the answer to this next question I give some tips to help you get the most benefit from reading your bible.

~~~

**Q.** Can the Bible be interpreted anyway you want?
Two related questions:
- What might be the checks on radically-subjective readings of the text?
- How should you read the Bible?

**A.** The Apostle Paul tells Timothy "Study to shew thyself approved unto God, a workman that needeth not to be ashamed, rightly dividing the word of truth" (2Timothy 2:15). From that verse alone it is easy to see that there is a RIGHT way to interpret scriptures, and it is just as easy to see that has not stopped anyone from misinterpreting it.

There is a system called hermeneutics or (a system of interpretation), which is helpful with interpreting scriptures. However, it is fallible and not designed to be a rigid set of rules because the "Word of God" is very much alive. God has spoken to many a believer through scriptures, to help us make certain decisions in life. However, these incidents are not things to build a doctrine on, nor used to lead a congregation. In my personal experience, they made sense to me at the time, and it is unlikely anyone else would have understood why I made the decision I did, even if I shared with them the scripture God *spoke* to me. I should also tell you that the results of some of those decisions have been far reaching and I may not ever know how far, or how important they are on this side of life. A simple kindness may turn a suicidal person around, or enable a drunkard, while being a hard ass may be a wakeup call to someone being a fool, or plant a bitter root in another person.

So how are we to know, when to be kind, and when to be tough?

I give up.

Without the guidance of the Holy Spirit, I cannot know what my decisions or actions might cause, I must admit sometimes I still miss, in such cases; all I can do is pray that God will turn my mess to His glory.

As for studying the scriptures, there are different types of studying and if you are truly serious about your quest I suggest getting a good King James Version (KJV) bible and a Strong's Exhaustive Concordance with the Greek and Hebrew Lexicons. The bible should be large clear print. If you want to get other versions of the bible that is fine too but the Strong's is designed to coincide with the KJV. I also recommend getting a good dictionary and keeping a notebook handy.

There are three scriptures you need to have faith in.

1. If ye then, being evil, know how to give good gifts unto your children, how much more shall your Father which is in heaven give good things to them that ask him? (Mathew 7:11).
2. Trust in the LORD with all thine heart; and lean not unto thine own understanding (Proverbs 3:5).
3. Whom shall he teach knowledge? and whom shall he make to understand doctrine? *them that are* weaned from the milk, *and* drawn from the breasts. For precept *must be* upon precept, precept upon precept; line upon line, line upon line; here a little, *and* there a little: For with stammering lips and another tongue will he speak to this people (Isaiah 28:9-11).

## Basic Hermeneutics *(a system of interpretation)*
## Eight helpful rules to follow

1. Always read the Old Testament in the light of the New Testament.
2. If God or Jesus said it then it is IMPORTANT, seek to know what it means.
3. The best interpretation of a particular book/chapter is the same book/chapter i.e. read things in the context they were written. *(Sometimes things can be lifted out as divine truths.)*
4. Scripture must support Scripture before you build a doctrine on it.
5. Research words and topics before coming to any conclusions.
6. Whenever you read the word "therefore" then back up and read the preceding text to see what it is "there for."

7.  The "rule of first mention," especially useful for topical studies. Going to the first time the subject is broached in scriptures to get a foundation to build on. Still you must look at it through number 1.
8.  The "rule of three," generally if something is found at least three times in scripture it becomes clear what it means.

### Types of Study

1.  Topical Study i.e. Salvation, Spiritual Gifts, Sin, Kingdom of God, hell, etc.
2.  Word Study i.e. Love, Blessing, Sorcery, etc. do not rely solely on an English dictionary.
3.  Prophesy; includes several fields of study.
    a.  Prophesies Fulfilled, (some knowledge of History is necessary)
    b.  End Times (pre-apocalypse)
    c.  Apocalypse

Remember the Father gives good gifts to those who ask, so do not forget to pray, (Mathew 7:11 *paraphrased*).

~~~

**Q.** What is the best text or video summary of the New Testament?

Hello, I'm generally curious, but alas I do not have the time to actually read and decipher the Bible, and I also have a sort of A.D.D. which makes it hard to concentrate on things that do not keep my attention.

**A.** I cannot really recommend any "summary" of the New Testament but if you are willing to at least read one of the Gospels I would recommend the gospel of Mark. It is the shortest of the gospels. Then read the shorter epistles some are only one chapter. Doing this should at least get you started and prick your interest to read other parts of the bible.

Other things you can do would be to pick up a "Through the Bible; Study Bible" that gives you a few sections to read every day. In a year, if you stick with it, you will have read it all. There is nothing saying you have to read it from cover to cover or within a certain amount of time.

Just do not let your A.D.D. become an excuse, think of it like this, if God exists then getting to know God should be of overriding importance and worthy of your time and attention. If God is a myth then any time lost to reading the Bible would probably have been wasted on something frivolous and less rewarding anyway.

~~~

**Q.** What should everyone know about the Bible?

**A.** The Bible:

1. Is the authoritative word from God to humanity.
2. Reveals the true nature of humanity.
3. Has practical advice for daily life.
4. Tells us of God's love for us.
5. Gives a warning of God's coming judgment.
6. Tells us of God's plan to save humanity from that Judgment.
7. Covers everything you need to know to develop a relationship with God.

~~~

**Q.** If God exist why hasn't he ever talked to me?

**A.** In most cases, it is because we do not come to Him properly. There are a few examples where Jesus demonstrates what gets God's attention in the Gospels. There is one very clear demonstration of approaching God that He will ignore.

First, what not to do...

In this event, a woman seeking a miracle for her daughter comes to Jesus. He ignores her and then basically calls the woman a dog after she persisted. It is not until she quits begging stands up and pushes the issue that Jesus tells her she has great faith.

First, she tries begging,

> And, behold, a woman of Canaan came out of the same coasts, and cried unto him, saying, Have mercy on me, O Lord, *thou* Son of David; my daughter is grievously vexed with a devil. But he answered her not a word. And his disciples came and besought him, saying, Send her away; for she crieth after us. But he answered and said, I am not sent but unto the lost sheep of the house of Israel (Mathew 15:22-24).

Next she tries *worship* which results in a word from the Lord but not an answer to prayer; in fact He calls her a dog;

> Then came she and worshipped him, saying, Lord, help me.

> But he answered and said, It is not meet to take the children's bread, and to cast *it* to dogs (Mathew 15:25-26).

Finally she asserts herself and her prayers are answered;

> And she said, Truth, Lord: yet the dogs eat of the crumbs which fall from their masters' table.
>
> Then Jesus answered and said unto her, O woman, great *is* thy faith: be it unto thee even as thou wilt. And her daughter was made whole from that very hour.

This may seem cruel at first glance but what Jesus did was teach this woman that being humble does not mean you should not be dignified.

Another time Jesus teaches a parable of an unjust judge, look at the similarities between how He treated that woman, and His parable.

> And he spake a parable unto them *to this end,* that men ought always to pray, and not to faint; Saying, There was in a city a judge, which feared not God, neither regarded man: And there was a widow in that city; and she came unto him, saying, Avenge me of mine adversary. And he would not for a while: but afterward he said within himself, Though I fear not God, nor regard man; Yet because this widow troubleth me, I will avenge her, lest by her continual coming she weary me(Luke 18:1-5).

Jesus explains why He taught this parable,

> And the Lord said, Hear what the unjust judge saith. And shall not God avenge his own elect, which cry day and night unto him, though he bear long with them? I tell you that he will avenge them speedily. Nevertheless when the Son of man cometh, shall he find faith on the earth? (Luke 18:6-8)

Notice that last line… Jesus is saying that even though His children are crying and desperate, or begging day and night, He does not recognize those approaches as using faith. But because God is a just and loving God He will still answer their prayers. Nevertheless, I believe a lot of people could have a much happier relationship with the Lord if they would stop whining, and start calling God out on His promises. After all Jesus said "~ I have come that you might have life and have it more abundantly" (John 10:10b)

Another mistake,

> And He spake this parable unto certain which trusted in themselves that they were righteous, and despised others: Two men went up into the temple to pray; the one a Pharisee, and the other a publican (Luke18:9-10).

Boasting in one's own piety,

> The Pharisee stood and prayed thus with himself, God, I thank thee, that I am not as other men *are,* extortioners, unjust, adulterers, or even as this publican. 12 I fast twice in the week, I give tithes of all that I possess(Luke 18:11-12).

Compared to this,

> And the publican, standing afar off, would not lift up so much as *his* eyes unto heaven, but smote upon his breast, saying, God be merciful to me a sinner.

> I tell you, this man went down to his house justified *rather* than the other: for every one that exalteth himself shall be abased; and he that humbleth himself shall be exalted (Luke 18:13-14).

Jesus makes it very clear in that parable that we are not to brag about what we are doing for Him. Jesus admires faith, use it and you will get results, study 1st Corinthians chapter 13 too. You will see that Love is greater than faith. Love is not boastful or proud. If Love therefore is meek, then how much more should we who walk by faith also be meek?

I mentioned some examples of the kind of faith that pleases God. I only listed a few, because I hope that you will continue to seek God in your own studies. The scriptures are filled with wonderful examples of how to get God's attention. I can assure you, He desires to know you more than you desire to know him.

The Centurion's Faith as told by Mathew.

> And when Jesus was entered into Capernaum, there came unto him a centurion, beseeching him, And saying, Lord, my servant lieth at home sick of the palsy, grievously tormented. And Jesus saith unto him, I will come and heal him (Mathew 8:5-7).

The centurion demonstrates both meekness and faith.

> The centurion answered and said, Lord, I am not worthy that thou shouldest come under my roof: but speak the word only, and my servant shall be healed. For I am a man under authority, having soldiers under me: and I say to this *man,* Go, and he goeth; and to another, Come, and he cometh; and to my servant, Do this, and he doeth *it.*
>
> When Jesus heard *it,* he marvelled, and said to them that followed, Verily I say unto you, I have not found so great faith, no, not in Israel. And I say unto you, That many shall come from the east and west, and

shall sit down with Abraham, and Isaac, and Jacob, in the kingdom of heaven. But the children of the kingdom shall be cast out into outer darkness: there shall be weeping and gnashing of teeth. And Jesus said unto the centurion, Go thy way; and as thou hast believed, *so* be it done unto thee. And his servant was healed in the selfsame hour (Mathew 8:8-13).

Luke's version of this story shows us that the centurion was wealthy, yet he still shows the same humility and faith as in Mathew's version. This tells us a great deal about this man's character.

Now when he had ended all his sayings in the audience of the people, he entered into Capernaum. And a certain centurion's servant, who was dear unto him, was sick, and ready to die. And when he heard of Jesus, he sent unto him the elders of the Jews, beseeching him that he would come and heal his servant.

And when they came to Jesus, they besought him instantly, saying, That he was worthy for whom he should do this: For he loveth our nation, and he hath built us a synagogue. Then Jesus went with them.

And when he was now not far from the house, the centurion sent friends to him, saying unto him, Lord, trouble not thyself: for I am not worthy that thou shouldest enter under my roof: Wherefore neither thought I myself worthy to come unto thee: but say in a word, and my servant shall be healed. For I also am a man set under authority, having under me soldiers, and I say unto one, Go, and he goeth; and to another, Come, and he cometh; and to my servant, Do this, and he doeth *it*.

When Jesus heard these things, he marvelled at him, and turned him about, and said unto the people that followed him, I say unto you, I have not found so great faith, no, not in Israel. And they that were sent, returning to the house, found the servant whole that had been sick (Luke 7:1-10).

In both versions of this story we see that this centurion was a leader used to giving orders. In Mathew's version, we see how he speaks with Jesus about his servant. There seems to be a pleading in his voice, but it is quite different from that of the Canaanite woman who was crying out. In Luke's version, the centurion had called some allies whom he had done favors for. I think Jesus had already made up His mind that He would heal the servant. However, another element is important. From what we read in Luke, the centurion was not bragging on himself and declaring his worthiness, but the elders of Judaism. It is a biblical principal to live a life in such a way that you are spoken well of before God and men, no easy task, but not impossible.

What made Jesus "marvel" at this man's faith? The man recognized that Jesus was a man of authority. He says, "Jesus, I give orders, and my servants and soldiers carry them out. All you have to do is give the order and your servant *(faith)* will heal my servant." Wow, what a concept he not only recognized the authority of Jesus but he fully expected it to happen.

This centurion's story is a wealth of insight to communicating with the Lord. He spoke to him with humility but still expected a result. He himself never made mention that he had built a synagogue, but his reputation spoke for him.

Now ask yourself, how do you approach the Lord?

Do you come begging like a dog? You are a person; try talking to Him instead. Believe it or not, He has a lot invested in you and He is interested in getting to know you.

Do you come proud? Do you think you are better than other people? You are not; you are not any better than anyone else. We are all sinners and our righteousness is no better than a filthy rag to Him. Yes, He loves you. You are valuable to Him but not for what you have done or for what you have. He loves the person He created you to be, to fulfill the purpose He has for you.

Are you worshiping Him with some religious practice or ritual? God is not moved by artificial worship. He desires that you worship Him in spirit and truth. "But the hour cometh, and now is, when the true worshippers shall worship the Father in spirit and in truth: for the Father seeketh such to worship him" (John 4:23).

He is willing to come to you if you are humble and recognize Him for whom He really is. The Lord Jesus Christ, the Son of the Living God, who died for your sins and arose again. "He stands at the door and knocks open your heart and He will come in" (Revelations 3:20).

~~~

**Q.** How do we know that The Bible wasn't tampered with by people in power who wanted to use the texts to their advantage?

**A.** The old adage of "knowledge is power," comes to mind. Some people do feel that way, so you are not the first one to come up with the idea. However, if you read and study the Bible for yourself you will find that it does more to liberate individuals, than it does to wield power over them. This liberating effect drove those who were in power to keep it out of the hands of the general populace for generations.

Ultimately, the Bible was written over several centuries as God gave revelation to His prophets. Its primary function is to lead people to Christ. Nevertheless, it can provide some very practical advice for life and for a believer it does much more.

1. It builds my faith in Christ (Romans 10:17)
2. Teaches me about Christ (Ephesians 3:19)
3. Teaches me about me (James 1:23)
4. Tells me how to please Christ (Hebrews 11:6, 2Timothy 2:4)
5. Liberates me from sin (Romans 6:18, 22, Galatians 5:1)
6. Promises me a hope and a future (Romans 8:24)
7. Warns me of deceivers (Mathew 24:24, Mark 13:22)

Those are just a few things that I find liberating me as opposed to oppressing me.

~~~

# Chapter 2

# Prayer

*"When we rely upon organization, we get what organization can do; when we rely upon education, we get what education can do; when we rely upon eloquence, we get what eloquence can do. And so on. But when we rely upon prayer, we get what God can do." A.C. Dixon*

1. How Can I Learn to Pray?
2. How do I get the emotional benefit of praying to God if I am an atheist?
3. Why don't all people who believe in prayer pray only for the good of everyone?
4. What are Christians who pray that God will "bless this food to our bodies" before meals asking for?

**Q.** How Can I Learn to Pray?

**A.** There are only three rules to prayer.

1.  Have a relationship with Jesus; believe that Jesus died and arose from death for your sins.
2.  Be humble; think about it, who are you to tell God how to get things done. Instead, study His word and allow Him to lead you and guide you.
3.  Be willing to obey God, the bible says, "The steps of a good man are ordered of the Lord" (Psalms 37:23).

You can ask the lord for anything, talk to Him about anything, but I would recommend that you begin by asking Him for understanding of His ways, what pleases him, etc. Many people make the mistake of trying to barter with God. I do not recommend that. It is likely you will fail on your end. It will not cost you your salvation, but you will have to answer for it. God does not play with an oath or a vow. If you make one and do not fulfill it, then it will cost you some reward at the judgment.

If He leads you to a Church then be faithful and go. If you are truly seeking God, He will help you find a place where you can grow in him.

Be grateful for He has saved you for all eternity; when you understand how great His salvation is you understand also that He is worthy of your praise.

Finally learn to hear from God and do not be afraid to ask Him to make things plain to you. He will show you what you need to understand in a way that you will understand. As you grow in the Lord, your prayers will become more effectual and so will your understanding. God longs to spend time with you and His ear is always prepared to listen. The answer to the next question may prove helpful in this.

~~~

**Q.** How do I get the emotional benefit of praying to God if I am an atheist?

I just wish someone could hear me. Maybe a psychotherapist I guess. If only I could pray to one.

**A.** Friend; God is listening; He is just waiting for you to say, "LORD JESUS i BELIEVE in YOU, come in to my heart." You do not really have to do anything more than keep believing and allow Him to work in you.

He will give you; "beauty for ashes, the oil of joy for mourning, the garment of praise for the spirit of heaviness; that you might be called a tree of righteousness, the planting of the LORD, that he might be glorified" (Isaiah 61:3).

I received these responses from that answer. The concern is legitimate so I thought I should include it even though it goes a different direction. Plus, it gives me an opportunity lead you through a word study on "repent."

**Response** "I have to disagree with you theologically. God must regenerate his heart. And He commands us not just to believe, but to REPENT."

**Me.** "I understand, but I believe that once a heart can believe the soul has already reached the place of repentance. Repentance is not remorse or regret but change, especially in thinking. Here is a word study from scripture where Jesus tells the Jews to repent."

I tell you, Nay: but, except ye **repent G3340**, ye shall all likewise perish (Luke 13:3).

According to Strong's Greek Lexicon

G3340
μετανοέω
metanoeō̄
met-an-o-eh'-o
From G3326 and G3539; to think differently or afterwards, that is, reconsider (morally to feel compunction): - repent.

Repentance is changing from unbelief to belief. For the heart to be able to say, "Jesus is Lord" requires a revelation from God. "Wherefore I give you to understand, that no man speaking by the Spirit of God calleth Jesus accursed: and that no man can say that Jesus is the Lord, but by the Holy Ghost" (1Corinthians 12:3).

There are three times when "repent" could have been interpreted as "having regret." Once in Hebrews when the author is speaking about God's decision to give us Christ, and twice in Second Corinthians.

For those priests were made without an oath; but this with an oath by him that said unto him, The Lord sware and will not repent G3338, Thou art a priest for ever after the order of Melchisedec (Hebrews 7:21).

For though I made you sorry with a letter, I do not repent G3338, though I did repent G3338: for I perceive that the same epistle hath made you sorry, though it were but for a season (2Corinthians 7:8).

According to Strong's Greek Lexicon this word comes from the Greek word metamellomai.

> G3338
> μεταμέλλομαι
> metamellomai
> met-am-el'-lom-ahee
> From G3326 and the middle of G3199; to care afterwards, that is, regret: - repent (self).

The true doctrine of biblical repentance is not to bring so much guilt that a person feels worthless, but to bring them to a place where they change their thinking about God. I understand about empty or dead faith and a passive acceptance that there exists a God is not saving faith. In the case of this atheist he truly wants to talk to a living God; all that is required is for him to change his thinking *(repent)* of what he believes about God's existence and the Gospel of Jesus. When he does, God will take over. For him to admit that Jesus is the risen Lord is an act of repentance *(change)*, it is he saying, "I was wrong."

God is not concerned about anyone's past sins He separates us from those when we accept Jesus as our Lord. People can be full of regret but without Jesus, it does not change anything. When Jesus called His disciples He did not set there and tell them what terrible sinners they were, but He did tell Peter that except He wash him, that he could have no place in the Lord. Peter instantly changed his thinking *(repented)* and said "Lord wash me all over."

Search out the Scripture my friend; going to the extreme of either doctrine does not make good disciples.

~~~

**Q.** Why don't all people who believe in prayer pray only for the good of everyone?

What prompted this question:

- I've heard people pray for their football team to win right after hearing someone else pray for their father to be healed of cancer.
- I wondered why anyone, who actually believed in the power of prayer, wouldn't always and only pray for all good things to happen to everyone.

**A.** Most of my prayers are a bit selfish. No I don't ask the Lord to make me rich beyond measure, nor do I pray, "Lord bless me, my wife, and our two kids, us four and no more," type of prayers. I pray, "Lord teach me to do what is right that I may be your light." Yes I desire to be a light of God. To speak truth and the wisdom of God in a dark earth, recently I have realized that just being a light does not mean that the darkness perceives it. So I also pray for the eyes of enlightenment to be opened as well. So my selfish prayers are not just for me but for everyone else too.

I don't usually pray for team "x" to win, but if I have a friend on a team I may pray for him/her and their team but that is because I am personally vested. So, yet another selfish prayer; yes?

I pray for the people of Haiti because God placed them in my heart, after I met a young Haitian woman who told me of the hardships there since the earthquake. So I pray for God's mercy and grace to manifest itself in a supernatural way to bring truth and blessing to all the people of Haiti.

I pray for criminals to be caught and stopped. I also pray that they come to the knowledge of Jesus Christ and turn from their evil ways and embrace the living way. I even pray for several of you who ask these questions. A lot of you are pretty smart folks, if God opens your eyes then you could all do wonderful things for the Kingdom of God.

Why do a lot of Christians pray for seemingly silly things? Usually it is because they are not mature in the Lord. But even if that is the case those small things God can use to do great things. When I say, "God moves in mysterious ways," it is not to make an excuse for why bad things happen. It is about His ability to turn an acorn into an oak forest. I think we sometimes look at the size of the problems and think we need a solution just as big. God often uses the tiniest things to solve big problems.

> *"We are like voices crying in the wilderness; we prepare the way for a glorious future. Future missionaries will be rewarded with conversions for every sermon. We are their pioneers and helpers. Let them not forget the watchman of the night - us who worked when all was gloom, and no evidence of success in the way of conversion cheered our paths. They will doubtless have more light than we; but we can serve our Master earnestly, and proclaim the Gospel, as they will do." David Livingstone, 11 November 1853*

~~~

**Q.** What are Christians who pray that God will "bless this food to our bodies" before meals asking for?

**A.** While most Christians are not aware of it the word 'bless' has an amazing meaning. In the Hebrew language, it is the word bârak.

H1288

ברך

bârak

baw-rak'

A primitive root; to kneel; by implication to bless God (as an act of adoration), and (vice-versa) man (as a benefit); also (by euphemism) to curse (God or the king, as treason): - X abundantly, X altogether, X at all, blaspheme, **bless**, congratulate, curse, X greatly, X indeed, kneel (down), praise, salute, X still, thank. *(Strong's Hebrew Lexicon)*

The word is twofold and double-edged. In general practice, we are asking God to do a good work. God does not do evil so asking God to curse something is absurd. So blessing the food is to ask God to make sure that it is set apart for us and clean, not tainted by idols and with me I add, "that it bring strength, health and healing to all who are about to partake."

~~~

# Chapter 3

# Morality

*"Wherever any precept of traditional morality is simply challenged to produce its credentials, as though the burden of proof lay on it, we have taken the wrong position."* C.S. Lewis

1. If God does not exist is everything permitted?
2. What is the origin of the phrase, "Know God in all your ways, even in sin?
3. Where in the bible does it say that sex outside marriage is sin?
4. If there is no God, why is killing people an immoral act?
5. How do homophobic religious people who believe homosexuality is wrong explain the presence of gay people in wholesome religious communities?
6. How do rich people justify not helping starving people more than they do?
7. Does god Exist? If yes, then why did he create religion, race, and caste, dividing Human beings amongst themselves?
8. Why was slavery not condemned by God or Jesus?
9. Does God totally reject established laws and institutions?
10. Why do humans have consciousness?
11. Is a person only a real Christian, Muslim etc. if they adhere to the word of their religion?
12. What is the power of words?

**Q.** If God does not exist is everything permitted?

What should one base morality on in the absence of God? If there are no strings attached and nothing exists after death, why not do immoral things?

**A.** I try never to use the "moral high ground" to argue the existence of God. Morality is relative and defined by the ruling class. If a society says it is ok to sacrifice little girls, then they will do so without fear. If a society says it is ok to abort pregnancies in the last trimester, then people will do so. If society decides it is ok for women to become fetal farms to advance stem cell research, they will do it.

Modern "Secular Humanism" has no anchor. They say we know it is wrong to murder, but ancient Romans glorified it with Gladiators. Of course, the Romans were not godless but worshiped idols that did not speak. They created the rules as it suited them. I see no reason why Secular Humanists would do any better.

Historically religions have not fared well as a moral guide. It is like a rubber crutch. The religious mind clings to rituals and rules established by humans. Once exposed as false, the followers may lose their sense of self and purpose. They may take their liberty to extremes, becoming the opposite of what they were taught, depending on how deeply they had bought into the deception. This is true even in religions that create an illusion of having good morals.

The Abrahamic religions claim they are "Established by God" and say we have the answers to society's problems and our morals are right because God says so. What they all fail to understand is that the path to God is not in establishing rules of moral behavior. The Bible teaches us that the laws in the Abrahamic faiths are indeed given by God; however, they expose our failures to show us that we cannot achieve any morality in our own power that is acceptable with God. The chart below shows that the only morality God accepts comes through a true relationship first.

| | | | |
|---|---|---|---|
| **A** | Morality - God | = | Failed Establishment |
| **B** | Morality + Religion | = | Failed Understanding = Failed Establishment |
| **C** | Morality + God | = | Failed Relationship = Failed Understanding = Failed Establishment |
| **D** | God + Nothing | >= | Morality + Relationship + Establishment + Understanding + Every Good Thing |

(A) Is true because the humans are inconsistent we are not carbon copies of one another and even if we have a written moral code or law it will change with each passing generation.

(B) Is true because religions are led by their oracles. They fall prey to the agenda of a few powerful people who will put that above their moral compass.

(C) Seems right but is where most people get confused. This is an attempt to live your life in such a way as to get God to accept you. Believe me I tried and found it impossible. The Bible says, "But we are all as an unclean *thing*, and all our righteousnesses *are* as filthy rags; and we all do fade as a leaf; and our iniquities, like the wind, have taken us away" (Isaiah 64:6).

(D) The path to a moral society is through God. This is what Jesus meant when He said, "But seek ye first the kingdom of God, and his righteousness; and all these things shall be added unto you" (Mathew 6:33). The only way to do that is to seek God and get to know Him personally. Ask Him what you need to do to be accepted by Him, study His word and allow Him to show you it's true meaning. In so doing you will find Him and discover the life, He has planned for you.

~~~

**Q.** What is the origin of the phrase, "Know God in all your ways, even in sin?

**A.** That saying is a twisted biblical phrase probably from Proverbs 3:6 "In all thy ways acknowledge him, and he shall direct thy paths."

The Bible does say that God knows us, even when we feel like we are so deep in sin we cannot escape it.

> If I ascend up into heaven, thou art there: if I make my bed in hell, behold, thou art there (Psalm 139:8).

> But he knoweth the way that I take: when he hath tried me, I shall come forth as gold (Job 23:10).

In this Scripture, it tells us that those who know Him also know the things that please Him.

> But let him that glorieth glory in this, that he understandeth and knoweth me, that I am the LORD which exercise lovingkindness, judgment, and righteousness, in the earth: for in these things I delight, saith the LORD (Jeremiah 9:24).

He also says that even while we are in sin, He loves us.

> But God commendeth his love toward us, in that, while we were yet sinners, Christ died for us (Romans 5:8).

> But God, who is rich in mercy, for his great love wherewith he loved us (Ephesians 2:4).

> Herein is love, not that we loved God, but that he loved us, and sent his Son to be the propitiation for our sins (1John 4:10).

> We love him, because he first loved us (1John 4:19).

So the biblical verse does not tie God to being a partaker of our sins but the path out of them.

~~~

**Q.** Where in the bible does it say that sex outside marriage is sin?

Without Christianity, I understand that those who are in power want to control and regulate others' sex life. Hence they want to be the pimp of all hoes. This explains why virtually most fascist religions oppose that too.

However, theologically is there anything that CLEARLY and DIRECLY prohibits sex outside marriage?

I am aware that:

1. Sex with mom, sister, other's wife, others' fiancée (because Jews count a fiancée as a wife) is illegal. That is not prohibition of sex outside marriage in GENERAL.
2. There are prohibitions against "sexual immorality." Again, this is NOT CLEAR what counts as sexual immorality.
3. There is also a prohibition against selling daughters to prostitution. Again, selling people is not legal anyway now so that's irrelevant.

**A.** The bible refers to sex outside of marriage as fornication and nowhere in scripture does the bible look favorably on it.

Jesus plainly said, "That whosoever looketh on a woman to lust after her hath committed adultery with her already in his heart" (Mathew 5:28).

Then the Apostle Paul writes to the Corinthians:

> 9 Know ye not that the unrighteous shall not inherit the kingdom of God? Be not deceived: neither fornicators, nor idolaters, nor adulterers, nor effeminate, nor abusers of themselves with mankind, 10 Nor thieves, nor covetous, nor drunkards, nor revilers, nor extortioners, shall inherit the kingdom of God.
>
> 11 And such were some of you: but ye are washed, but ye are sanctified, but ye are justified in the name of the Lord Jesus, and by the Spirit of our God.
>
> 12 All things are lawful unto me, but all things are not expedient: all things are lawful for me, but I will not be brought under the power of any (1Corinthians 6:9-12).

This tells me that although any of those behaviors will not cost you your salvation they will cost you kingdom privileges now in this life and in the life to come. If you pursue them, you come under the power and snare of sin. If you have believed the bible and have accepted Jesus into your heart then you would understand that having casual sex is not pleasing to God.

~~~

**Q.** If there is no God, why is killing people an immoral act?

If humanity exists by some sort of accident with no particular plan or purpose.

**A.** In human societies, murder is only immoral if the ruling class says it is. Many of the ancient pagans regularly sacrificed their children especially baby girls who were considered less valuable to society than boys were. Most of these sacrifices were done in the name of some god. Often, the prominent people in those societies would have their slaves sacrificed when they died so they could have servants in the afterlife. To them it was the natural way of things.

Not all senseless killings were for religious purposes, I am sure you have heard about the Roman Gladiators. The socially accepted in Roman culture is considered very immoral in the US and most developed countries in our modern world.

The following shows that the Romans considered killing or dying in the arena a very socially acceptable event.

> Irrespective of their origin, gladiators offered spectators an example of Rome's martial ethics and, in fighting or dying well they could inspire admiration and popular acclaim. They were celebrated in high and low art, and their value as entertainers was commemorated in precious and commonplace objects throughout the Roman world. *(http://en.wikipedia. org/wiki/Gladiator)*

Has humanity improved? We tend to think we are civilized but even today there are a great deal of human sacrifices, only now it is not a religious exercise or sport. It is for greed. Drug cartels in many countries around the world feel they are completely justified for killing anyone who trespasses or otherwise gets in the way of their agenda. Murder is not the worst of immoral acts being practiced today. The love of money is again at the root of human trafficking.

All of these evils have been occurring for thousands of years now. If anything, we have gotten better at killing which makes us worse than our predecessors. Judaic based faiths are often criticized for worshiping a wrathful God but it is not God who authored sin and confusion. The Christian bible I believe has proven to be a true guide to a good God, who is continually seeking to turn humans from our ways to His. His will for us… "Beloved, I wish above all things that thou mayest prosper and be in health, even as thy soul prospereth" (3John 1:2).

In the next question, I explain in a bit more detail why Christians should not try to use moral ideology to convince people to believe in Jesus.

~~~

**Q.** How do homophobic religious people who believe homosexuality is wrong explain the presence of gay people in wholesome religious communities?

What environmental factors do they believe have caused those people to become gay? Surely, there is nothing within these heterosexual societies to corrupt anyone?

To clarify, I am not suggesting ALL religious people are homophobic. Please do not read a generalization where there is not one.

**A.** Your question/statement is an oxymoron; phobias of any kind are not healthy so it is reasonable to assume that a phobic personality would be so obsessed with the phobia that they seek it out and draw it to themselves. It is possible that those who are most vocal about homosexuality could be struggling with temptations and trying to talk themselves out of it. This of course does nothing to nurture the healthy relationship they consciously want but feeds the unhealthy desire to the point they fall or cause those close to them to fall into the sin. I do see homosexuality as sin but that does not make them excluded from God's love or mercy. God is able to deliver anyone from sin when, they turn to Him and away from trusting their own ways.

I think the subliminal question here is whether homosexuality is nature or nurture. I used to think it was a choice and to some degree, I still believe that; however, over the years of meditating on God's word and asking Him why these things happen I have realized that sin has caused genetic defects. Science calls this evolution and of course, they would claim the process is advancing the species over lots of trial and error and the strongest survives. My personal view is that evolution is a degenerative struggle for survival in a world separated from God. Its effect and influence in nature is quite evident and it requires a very obstinate mind to ignore this evidence.

I said all that to make the point that it is possible that a person could be born with a genetic defect. I am not a scientist so I cannot disclaim the possibility however; this life style is still a choice. The argument that no one would choose it does not hold water; people make bad choices all the time. The good news is that even after years of making bad choices some have turned around and left those things behind, embracing Jesus and a much healthier lifestyle. So can you.

The argument for nurture states that, "when children are raised properly they will not become homosexuals." The problem with that thinking is that the very best parents are flawed and people are unique at birth. This means that even the most loving, God-fearing parents are going to make mistakes and sometimes those mistakes can have damaging effects on their children. What they believe they are doing right is not always so. Second problem is that no parent can shield his or her children from the realities of a flawed world. Ultimately, sin of any kind can infect anyone's life if they allow it too. The Good news is that Jesus can deliver anyone who calls out to him.

~~~

**Q.** How do rich people justify not helping starving people more than they do?

Some wealthy people decide to buy a 20th car or a 10th house instead of feeding a poor village. I'm wondering if it crosses their mind that they can use their money to prevent starvation instead of on (what seems to me like) gross self-indulgence.

If the possibility of helping struggling people does occur to a rich spender, what are they thinking when they decide not to do it?

**A.** The real problem is not whether or not the wealthy should give to the poor they will justify themselves in their own eyes. How do corrupt governments, charities and Christian organizations justify themselves for exploiting the poor? Again, they justify themselves, they are convinced that they are more deserving than the poor. "The poorest people in America are giving money to the wealthiest people in Haiti" *(Timothy T Schwartz Ph.D. Travesty in Haiti: A true account of Christian missions, orphanages, fraud, food aid and drug trafficking)*.

To change the world a people will have to turn from self, seek the face of God, and pray. (2Chronicles 7:14 paraphrased) You see it really does not work just to give, and give, even when you give to someone you know if it is not done in Love, it will not change much. To change the world you first need to allow God to change you. Below is an outline I made of 1Corinthians 13 from the Literal Translation Bible (LITV).

### *The Gifts of Spirit vs. Love*

> 1 If I speak with the tongues of men and of angels, but I do not have love, I have become as sounding brass or a clanging cymbal. 2 And if I have prophecies, and know all mysteries and all knowledge, and if I have all faith so as to move mountains, but do not have love, I am nothing.

### *Self-Sacrifice vs. Love*

> 3 And if I give out all my goods, and if I deliver my body that I be burned, but I do not have love, I am not profited anything.

### *Love's Attributes*

> 4 Love has patience, is kind; love is not envious; love is not vain, is not puffed up; 5 does not behave indecently, does not pursue its own things, is not easily provoked, thinks no evil; 6 does not rejoice in unrighteousness, but rejoices in the truth. 7 Love quietly covers all things, believes all things, hopes all things, endures all things.

### *Love's Supremacy over the Spiritual Gifts*

> 8 Love never fails. But if there are prophecies, they will be caused to cease; if tongues, they shall cease; if knowledge, it will be caused to cease. 9 For we know in part, and we prophesy in part; 10 but when the

perfect thing comes, then that which is in part will be caused to cease.

### What is Temporary vs. what is Eternal

11 When I was an infant, I spoke as an infant, I thought as an infant, I reasoned as an infant. But when I became a man, I caused to cease the things of the infant. 12 For now we see through a mirror in dimness, but then face to face. Now I know in part, but then I will fully know even as I also was fully known. 13 And now faith, hope, and love, these three things remain; but the greatest of these is love.

Some people use verse three as an excuse not to give, but they miss the point. One who has Love residing in them, will display the Gifts of the Spirit including the gift of giving. It is the gift of giving that is both effectual, and infectious giving. Have you ever seen the movie, "Pay it Forward?" It is a fictitious example of infectious giving, but I have seen real examples in churches where money was going directly to a specific cause.

So rather than concern about the wealth of some; as if they could change the world, seek the Lord to be infectious wherever He leads you and in every good work.

~~~

**Q.** Does god Exist? If yes, then why did he create religion, race, and caste, dividing Human beings amongst themselves?

If God exists, then I believe that He has created Religion, Caste, Race, etc. And these are the root cause of all the social evils, wars, discrimination and terrorism.

**A.** If I understand this question you are not sure of God's existence, but if he does then you want to blame Him for the state of the world. Let me see if I can show you what is really happening. I do believe God exists and while I believe He made Man, I understand that it is man that created the state of the world. According to the Bible God made man in His own image.

Rather than go the usual route of theology let's think for a minute about what God put in Man. God is good, so man was good. God is benevolent, so humans have this capacity also. Now I could go on and on about this but to get to the point that whatever is a part of God is also in us.

When Man fell in the Garden of Eden, all the goodness and godliness that was in Man became polluted. In the early days after the fall, many people still carried the attributes of God which may have even included the miraculous abilities that Jesus and many of the prophets displayed. Although they were greatly diminished, because of the evil presence that was growing in the hearts of all men. Imagine if God had allowed humans to reach the tree of life with such abilities coupled with a capacity or rather a propensity to do evil. Living forever and getting more and more evil with no means to cure yourself from sin. To me death is more merciful.

I know you would like to think that over time we would eventually start choosing to do well, but I have yet to see that last for very long. We try to force peace through might, but this generally winds up with the powerful abusing the weak. Even after all these millennium we still have people whose hearts are turned to do more evil than good and with no purpose for it.

So, if this is all true, then why does God even bother to save us? This has been a discussion for a millennium all its own. I believe that what God put in us, "the good" is still there. Humans have the ability to choose whether they will follow good that dwells in us, or the evil that entices us. The Bible tells us that God searches the hearts of all men. He is searching for something that to Him is of utmost value, which is the Light of men that was with Him in the beginning. "In him was life; and the life was the light of men" (John 1:4). Our capacity to follow the "good" on our own accord is still far short of what God put in us. It takes the Blood of Jesus to wash away the pollution and eventually bring us back into full fellowship with God.

I think that in spite of all the ordeals that humans go through, in the end and by the blood of Jesus, God will restore our former state to better than before we fell. We will then understand what evil is but it will no longer tempt us.

~~~

**Q.** Why was slavery not condemned by God or Jesus?

Was Jesus afraid to say, "Hey everybody, commandment #1 no more slavery! You can't own your fellow children of God, only God can!" Why isn't that in the text? Jesus is supposedly upset at what's going on in the temple, but not upset that humans own other humans? Did Jesus say to himself, "I'd like to say that and save a lot of people torment, but they'd never buy it so I'm keeping my mouth shut." This was the guy who was supposedly willing to go to the cross for what he said. He just punked out? What revelation is there? Wasn't Jesus supposed to reveal the new way of life, the new Christian ethic?

Didn't God know that people would justify slavery based on what's in the Old Testament and New Testament? Didn't Jesus have the foresight to know that he should explicitly condemn slavery so that there would be "divine" record of this? A condemnation of slavery in the Sermon on the Mount seems logical.

Heck, why didn't God make it part of the Ten Commandments. There'd be no reason to state "You shall not covet your neighbor's… male or female slave." Here's what should have been said, "I am the Lord your God, who brought you out of the land of Egypt, out of the house of slavery; **therefore you shall make slaves of no man, male or female**." God has a problem with the Egyptians having Hebrew slaves, but no qualms with slavery in general.

**A.** To begin with, God's commandments are rarely followed so it is not likely that the one you suggest would be either. Nevertheless, from the beginning of Man's fall, God has strove to guide him to truth and righteousness, "And the LORD said, My spirit shall not always strive with man, for that he also is flesh: yet his days shall be an hundred and twenty years" (Genesis 6:3). Your life is a gift from God and from the time you are born the Spirit of God has been calling you, it is up to you to stop and listen. He says, "Behold, I stand at the door, and knock: if any man hear my voice, and open the door, I will come in to him, and will sup with him, and he with me" (Rev 3:20).

Slavery is not man's invention but is one of the very attribute of God. Jesus said He came not to be served but to serve and yet He is the master. This mystery goes way over my head; however, I can tell you that the atrocity of slavery is not the relationship God ordained between a servant and a master.

God foretold that His people would know what the worst kind of slavery was, (Exodus 1:8-14). This was not something God took any pleasure in but saw the necessity of allowing it so that when he delivered them he could show the whole world how he would deal with people who oppressed others. (See Exodus 3:9, Exodus 22:21, Exodus 23:9, Leviticus 25:14, 17 and more I have put below)

I have read claims that slavery in ancient times was somewhat more tame and palatable than the slavery that was practiced in the New World, (the Colonial Americas). Try telling that to the women whose children were murdered for population control (Exodus 1:15-22). Another comment stated, "The Bible was *"written"* during time periods when many acts (spousal abuse, child abuse, torture, etc.) were not only commonplace, but were accepted social constructs."(sic) This may have been the case but the scriptures do not condone any such practices. To get to the heart of this let us look at the slavery of God's people in the scriptures.

### God's People Have Been Enslaved

> 8 Now there arose up a new king over Egypt, which knew not Joseph. 9 And he said unto his people, Behold, the people of the children of Israel *are* more and mightier than we: 10 Come on, let us deal wisely with them; lest they multiply, and it come to pass, that, when there falleth out any war, they join also unto our enemies, and fight against us, and *so* get them up out of the land. 11 Therefore they did set over them taskmasters to afflict them with their burdens. And they built for Pharaoh treasure cities, Pithom and Raamses. 12 But the more they afflicted them, the more they multiplied and grew. And they were grieved because of the children of Israel. 13 And the Egyptians made the children of Israel to serve with rigour: 14 And they made their lives bitter with hard bondage, in morter, and in brick, and in all manner of service in the field: all their service, wherein they made them serve, *was* with rigour (Exodus 1:8-14).

I know that only reads as a single paragraph, but the reality was several hundred years in which two wealthy cities had been built on the backs of slave labor. This easy life for the Egyptians would not be easy to give up, but they didn't stop with just forced labor. Fear of a revolt caused them to begin a cruel method of population control. Most people find this passage appalling.

### *The Pharaoh orders the murder of every newborn Hebrew male:*

> And the king of Egypt spake to the Hebrew midwives, of which the name of the one *was* Shiphrah, and the name of the other Puah: 16And he said, When ye do the office of a midwife to the Hebrew women, and see *them* upon the stools; if it *be* a son, then ye shall kill him: but if it *be* a daughter, then she shall live. 17 But the midwives feared God, and did not as the king of Egypt commanded them, but saved the men children alive. 18 And the king of Egypt called for the midwives, and said unto them, Why have ye done this thing, and have saved the men children alive? 19 And the midwives said unto Pharaoh, Because the Hebrew women *are* not as the Egyptian women; for they *are* lively, and are delivered ere the midwives come in unto them. 20 Therefore God dealt well with the midwives: and the people multiplied, and waxed very mighty. 21 And it came to pass, because the midwives feared God, that he made them houses. 22 And Pharaoh charged all his people, saying, Every son that is born ye shall cast into the river, and every daughter ye shall save alive (Exodus 1:15-22).

I agree those were some appalling conditions.

The inquisitor asks, "why didn't God just write the commandment don't own slaves?"

God did tell them to emancipate runaways, and provide a safe haven for them within their cities. Check these verses,

> Now therefore, behold, the cry of the children of Israel is come unto me: and I have also seen the oppression wherewith the Egyptians oppress them (Exodus 3:9).

> Thou shalt neither vex a stranger, nor oppress him: for ye were strangers in the land of Egypt (Exodus 22:21).

> Also thou shalt not oppress a stranger: for ye know the heart of a stranger, seeing ye were strangers in the land of Egypt (Exodus 23:9).

> And if thou sell ought unto thy neighbour, or buyest *ought* of thy neighbour's hand, ye shall not oppress one another: (Leviticus 25:14).

> Ye shall not therefore oppress one another; but thou shalt fear thy God: for I *am* the LORD your God (Leviticus 25:17).

> Thou shalt not oppress an hired servant *that is* poor and needy, *whether he be* of thy brethren, or of thy strangers that *are* in thy land within thy gates: (Deuteronomy 24:14).

God declares Emancipation:

> Thou shalt not deliver unto his master the servant which is escaped from his master unto thee: He shall dwell with thee, *even* among you, in that place which he shall choose in one of thy gates, where it liketh him best: thou shalt not oppress him (Deuteronomy 23:15-16).

Your question asks, "Did Jesus "Punk Out""?

Jesus said He himself came to serve.

> And there was also a strife among them, which of them should be accounted the greatest.
>
> And he said unto them, The kings of the Gentiles exercise lordship over them; and they that exercise authority upon them are called benefactors. But ye shall not be so: but he that is greatest among you, let him be as the younger; and he that is chief, as he that doth serve. For whether is greater, he that sitteth at meat, or he that serveth? is not he that sitteth at meat? but I am among you as he that serveth (Luke 22:24-27).

What he was saying is that a Godly master is one that carries the burdens of those that serve Him. I do not think he really wanted anyone owning anyone else, but he knows that we learn from what is in our environment I think he left things as such so we could grow. He also knows that this present world will end and that this life is temporary. The joy in the life to come will overshadow the evils of this brief one.

~~~

**Q.** Does God totally reject established laws and institutions?

**A.** No, the Bible teaches us to obey the law of the land. The only exception would be a law that prevented the spreading of the word of God. Christians can claim citizenship of their homeland and work towards changing those laws as they see fit. It doesn't mean they will be successful and it doesn't always mean that

Christians *(even true Christians)* are trying to establish good laws. You are asking about God and from everything I know about Him, He desires peace and order. With that being said, He recognizes that a spiritual war is going on, and He desires to save us from eternal losses, more than he desires peace on Earth. Everything He does is towards accomplishing this great commission of spreading the Gospel of Jesus Christ.

~~~

**Q.** Why do humans have consciousness?

The question is asked with consciousness defined as being aware of what one is thinking and doing. Why are humans the only thing on earth with the level of consciousness to have abstract thoughts, to see and predict what is not physical, and to believe what may not be true?

Please note that this isn't a question that so much can have an absolute answer, as is the case for most "why" questions. If anything, it is asking for what your life experience have led you to believe.

**A.** The reason is twofold, mainly that we are made in the Image of God, and were given a "Living Soul." But, it was not until Adam rebelled that our eyes were opened. With the knowledge of good and evil also came the self-awareness. Hopefully this outline will shed a little light on this subject.

### Man's design and purpose

And God said, Let us make man in our image, after our likeness: and let them have dominion over the fish of the sea, and over the fowl of the air, and over the

cattle, and over all the earth, and over every creeping
thing that creepeth upon the earth (Genesis 1:26).

### *God's breath of life makes him unique from all other creatures*

And the LORD God formed man of the dust of the
ground, and breathed into his nostrils the breath of
life; and man became a living soul (Genesis 2:7).

### *Man sins and becomes self-aware*

For God doth know that in the day ye eat thereof,
then your eyes shall be opened, and ye shall be as
gods, knowing good and evil. And when the woman
saw that the tree was good for food, and that it was
pleasant to the eyes, and a tree to be desired to make
one wise, she took of the fruit thereof, and did eat,
and gave also unto her husband with her; and he did
eat. And the eyes of them both were opened, and they
knew that they were naked; and they sewed fig leaves
together, and made themselves aprons (Genesis 3:5-7).

~~~

**Q.** Is a person only a real Christian, Muslim etc. if they adhere to
the word of their religion?

For instance, I have heard Christians say those who bomb
abortion clinics are not real Christians, or Muslims say the
same about Muslims who are terrorists. Those are the extremes
though, at what point of living outside of a religions tenets does
a person cease being considered a member of that religion?

**A.** People will self-identify as Christian, Muslim, Buddhist, or whatever, upon hearing that other people will identify them based on their perception of the tag. For example when I tell people I am a Christian, they may behave differently; some will constantly apologize for using language that they think offends me. Most of the time it does not and language that does offend me is another topic. More than a few times when I have told people I am a Christian, they immediately get defensive, thinking I am judging them right where they stand and act as if I can read their thoughts, and know every bad thing they ever did. Well I do not go round judging people, I do not care about what bad things you have done, and I cannot read minds. Nevertheless, when people who do evil things in the name of Jesus or Christianity I feel pretty sure that these people do not know the same Jesus I know.

The Bible tells us we can detect the true from the false, by the fruits they bare.

> Ye shall know them by their fruits. Do men gather grapes of thorns, or figs of thistles? Even so every good tree bringeth forth good fruit; but a corrupt tree bringeth forth evil fruit. A good tree cannot bring forth evil fruit, neither can a corrupt tree bring forth good fruit. Every tree that bringeth not forth good fruit is hewn down, and cast into the fire. Wherefore by their fruits ye shall know them. (Mathew 7:16-20)

To make this even simpler the Bible tells us what the fruit of Christian faith should be, compared to the works of human desires.

> Now the works of the flesh are manifest, which are these; Adultery, fornication, uncleanness, lasciviousness, Idolatry, witchcraft, hatred, variance,

emulations, wrath, strife, seditions, heresies, Envyings, murders, drunkenness, revellings, and such like: of the which I tell you before, as I have also told you in time past, that they which do such things shall not inherit the kingdom of God.

But the fruit of the Spirit is love, joy, peace, longsuffering, gentleness, goodness, faith, Meekness, temperance: against such there is no law.

And they that are Christ's have crucified the flesh with the affections and lusts. If we live in the Spirit, let us also walk in the Spirit. Let us not be desirous of vain glory, provoking one another, envying one another (Galatians 5:19-26).

And again in Ephesians

(For the fruit of the Spirit is in all goodness and righteousness and truth;) Proving what is acceptable unto the Lord. And have no fellowship with the unfruitful works of darkness, but rather reprove them (Ephesians 5:9-11)

~~~

**Q.** What is the power of words?

Past or present, in your life or for the masses, how have words made a difference?

**A.** *"I would rather play with forked lightning, or take in my hand living wires with their fiery current, than speak a reckless word against any servant of Christ, or idly repeat the slanderous*

*darts which thousands of Christian are hurling on others."*
*A.B. Simpson*

Words, right words and wrong words have a very powerful impact on hearers. Words have changed the course of events.

One such event occurred when a ship that was badly damaged and barely afloat was offered an opportunity for surrender but instead John Paul Jones cried out,

"Sir, I have only just begun to fight."

**Battle between the Serapis and Bonhomme Richard by Richard Paton, published 1780**

After his crew, who were exhausted, heard the captain's courageous words pushed on and latched onto the enemy vessel and took it captive, forcing it to surrender.

This is just one example of the power of words. Bitter words have started wars and better words ended them in treaties. So, it is with little wonder then that the Bible has so much to say about words.

Jesus said, "Every idle word that men shall speak, they shall give account thereof in the day of judgment. For by thy words thou shalt be justified, and by thy words thou shalt be condemned" (Mathew 12:36-37).

James said that, "The tongue is such a little member but it can set fire the whole course of nature." He then went further and said it is set on course to hell, (James 3:5-6).

Indeed words have caused riots; they have evoked lynchings, caused chaos and confusion. They have deceived just men, sent innocent men to prison and even death. They are used to swindle naive people out of their money and pervert truth to lies and make lies sound like truth.

Right words have brought peace to the hearer, invoked deeper thoughts. The Bible says, "A wholesome tongue *is* a tree of life: but perverseness therein *is* a breach in the spirit." (Proverbs 15:4)

Yet for all the power in the tongue, the Bible still says that God chose the foolishness of preaching to spread the Gospel.

> For Christ sent me not to baptize, but to preach the gospel: not with wisdom of words, lest the cross of Christ should be made of none effect. For the preaching of the cross is to them that perish foolishness; but unto us which are saved it is the power of God. For it is written, I will destroy the wisdom of the wise, and will bring to nothing the understanding of the prudent. Where is the wise? where is the scribe? where is the disputer of this world? hath not God made foolish the

wisdom of this world? For after that in the wisdom of God the world by wisdom knew not God, it pleased God by the foolishness of preaching to save them that believe (1Corinthians 1:17-21).

~~~

# Chapter 4

# Christianity

*"The basic trouble with the church today is her unworthy concept of God... Our religion is weak because our God is weak... Christianity at any given time is strong or weak depending on her concept of God." A.W. Tozer*

1. Did Jesus create Christianity?
2. Why doesn't the Bible mention the destruction of Pompeii?
3. Does Christianity have culture, tradition and ritualistic principles as people in Hindu, Islam and Buddhism follow?
4. What is the significance of the lamb in Christianity?
5. Does the New Testament say anything negative about Jews?
6. How and why did drumming and dancing come to be regarded as sinful in American Christianity?
7. Is it ok to work on the Sabbath?
8. I've heard the phrase "God between the gaps." If God exists but doesn't interfere with the Natural World, could He still be meaningful to humans in any practical way? If so; how?
9. Does God save people who are not Christians?
10. If Christian Catechism is true in stating that God created man to, "know Him, love Him and serve Him" then why does a perfect being need to be loved and served?
11. Why don't Christian women cover their head?
12. How can you know that you are saved?
13. Has there ever been any discussion amongst the leaders of the major Christian denominations about merging?
14. According to the bible, is it a sin for men to have long hair?
15. Why are you a Christian?

16. What is God to you?
17. Does God give preferential treatment to people who believe in His existence? If so; why?
18. What would you consider to be your life verse(s)" or "life scripture(s)" and why?
19. What are your core beliefs as a Christian?
20. Why do so many theists care what atheists believe?
21. Why are Christians concerned so much about what Jesus talked about the least in the bible?
22. How is a person saved (know they are going to heaven)?
23. Will the meek truly inherit the Earth?

**Q.** Did Jesus create Christianity?

**A.** Yes, Jesus created Christianity, however not until after His resurrection. He spent three and a half years training eleven handpicked individuals to spread the gospel of the kingdom. Then just before He departed from Earth He told them to wait for the Holy Spirit to come and give them power. His last words to them before He left were...

> All power is given unto me in heaven and in earth. Go ye therefore, and teach all nations, baptizing them in the name of the Father, and of the Son, and of the Holy Ghost: Teaching them to observe all things whatsoever I have commanded you: and, lo, I am with you alway, *even* unto the end of the world. Amen. (Mathew 28:18-20)

~~~

**Q.** Does Christianity have culture, tradition and ritualistic principles as people in Hindu, Islam and Buddhism follow? If yes what are best sources to explore?

**A.** There are many sects of Christianity that do have a lot of traditions, however the Lord said God desires us to worship Him in Spirit and Truth.

Jesus warns us not to follow the traditions of men, who think they are being holy and pleasing god through some ritual.

> 46 Beware of the scribes, which desire to walk in long robes, and love greetings in the markets, and the highest seats in the synagogues, and the chief rooms at feasts; 47 Which devour widows' houses, and for a

shew make long prayers: the same shall receive greater damnation (Luke 20:46-47).

6 Jesus answered and said unto them, Well hath Esaias prophesied of you hypocrites, as it is written, This people honoureth me with their lips, but their heart is far from me. 7 Howbeit in vain do they worship me, teaching for doctrines the commandments of men.

8 For laying aside the commandment of God, ye hold the tradition of men, as the washing of pots and cups: and many other such like things ye do. 9 And he said unto them, Full well ye reject the commandment of God, that ye may keep your own tradition (Mark 7:6-9).

Once when Jesus was speaking to a woman by a well of water and after some exchange of conversation he tells her:

23 But the hour cometh, and now is, when the true worshippers shall worship the Father in spirit and in truth: for the Father seeketh such to worship him. 24 God is a Spirit: and they that worship him must worship him in spirit and in truth (John 4:23-24).

You can read the full account in John 4, the whole chapter.

~~~

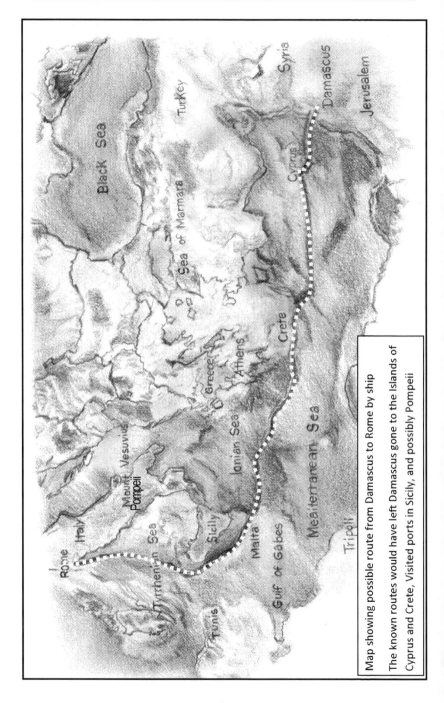

Map showing possible route from Damascus to Rome by ship

The known routes would have left Damascus gone to the Islands of Cyprus and Crete, Visited ports in Sicily, and possibly Pompeii

**Q.** Why doesn't the Bible mention the destruction of Pompeii?

**A.** Pompeii was destroyed around 79 A.D. The Old Testament had been written and the New Testament was in progress. Many Scholars believe that the gospels were not written until after 70 AD, (approximately 35-50 years after Christ was crucified) and those writings were focused on the life and ministry of Jesus. The epistles were written to the various churches. If there was a Church in Pompeii it would have been destroyed with the city.

From what archeologists have dug up the residents were primarily pagan worshipers and had likely rejected the gospel. The only thing Christian or Jewish that has been found at the site was some writing on a wall that said "Sodom and Gomorrah." It is believed someone who knew the scriptures also visited the site wrote this after its destruction. (The Day the World Ended: Lessons From Pompeii; http://www. ucg. org/news-and-prophecy/day-world-ended-lessons-pompeii/)

~~~

**Q.** What is the significance of the lamb in Christianity?

Through popular hymns such as Lamb of God, Jesus is the lamb, etc... What is the significance of the lamb?

**A.** During the "Feast of the Passover," just before the pharaoh allowed the Hebrew children go free; God instructed all the Hebrews to sacrifice a perfect lamb and apply its blood to the doorposts and lintels as a sign that they believed God. Then the families were to thoroughly cook and eat the entire lamb leaving nothing. The next day they were allowed to go and the Bible says there was not a feeble one among them. The essentials from this story include God working a miracle by healing everyone who followed the instructions and then He delivered them from slavery.

God told them never forget that day, so He ordained a special holiday to commemorate it. The purpose was so it would carry down through the ages. Every practicing Jew knows the story, they recognize that after a similar fashion, God will send a messiah that will deliver them and set up an everlasting kingdom on Earth.

What Jews fail to recognize is that God has already sent the messiah. Christians recognize Him in the person of Jesus whose blood was poured out and placed over the doorposts and lintels of our hearts so that in the last day we will be passed over when the whole Earth is judged. What the Jews practice to commemorate their deliverance from slavery a few thousand years ago is a figure of Christ who has become the eternal and everlasting lamb for our healing and our soul's deliverance and passage into God's kingdom forever.

~~~

**Q.** Does the New Testament say anything negative about Jews?

Why do most Christians hate Jews?

**A.** I am somewhat reluctant to answer this question because of the frequency which scriptures are used (out of context) to prop up some agenda. So again, I warn that anyone doing this is guilty of breaking the third commandment, using the Lord's name in vain.

Throughout history, anti-Semitic doctrine has been built from phrases from the New Testament for political purposes.

Paul wrote, "As concerning the gospel, they *(Jews)* are enemies for your sakes." If I wanted to get a bunch of naive people to hate the Jews I could take those words and build a case of how the Jews demanded Jesus be crucified. Then I could read the story in Mark chapter 15 where given the choice between Barabbas and Jesus, both of whom were charged with insurrection, they chose to let Barabbas free who not only was guilty of insurrection but also murdered for his cause. But, you see I sat here and misquoted something. I purposefully misquoted Romans 11:28 by leaving out half of the verse and not even showing you where it is found because in order to make this work I must also depend on your ignorance of scriptures. I am banking on the fact you are illiterate and trusting me to interpret God's word for your good.

Now all that is left for me to do is create my own rhetoric against the Jews and in order to ally yourself with God, you will call them your enemy and treat them as such.

So what does Romans 11:28 really say, "As concerning the gospel, they are enemies for your sakes: but as touching the election, they are beloved for the fathers' sakes."

What did Paul mean?

He meant that if following Judaism and Jewish traditions and doctrines could save us then the Gospel is worthless and Christ died for nothing. But because the Jews are the chosen vessel in which God was able to raise up prophets so that they through their prophesies could usher in the Messiah then God will one day bring them into the knowledge of Christ.

Now let us look at the passage in context.

> 25 For I would not, brethren, that ye should be ignorant of this mystery, lest ye should be wise in your own conceits; that blindness in part is happened to Israel, until the fulness of the Gentiles be come in.

26 And so all Israel shall be saved: as it is written,
There shall come out of Sion the Deliverer, and shall
turn away ungodliness from Jacob: 27 For this *is* my
covenant unto them, when I shall take away their sins.

**28** As concerning the gospel, *they are* enemies for your
sakes: but as touching the election, *they are* beloved for
the fathers' sakes. 29 For the gifts and calling of God
*are* without repentance.

30 For as ye in times past have not believed God, yet
have now obtained mercy through their unbelief:

31 Even so have these also now not believed, that
through your mercy they also may obtain mercy
(Romans 11:25-31).

Look at verse 31, "that through the mercy of Christians shall the
Jews obtain mercy" (paraphrased). This is hardly an anti-Semitic
teaching; rather it is one in where Christians are supposed to show
the Love of God so powerfully, that the natural Jew seeing it will
come to the knowledge of the truth of Jesus' gospel.

Compare that with verse 25, "to be ignorant of this mystery might make
you wise in your own conceits" (paraphrased). Anti-Semitism is based on
human conceits not the New Testament or the Gospel of Jesus Christ.

~~~

**Q.** How and why did drumming and dancing come to be regarded
as sinful in American Christianity?

Various Christian sects in America have banned drums and/
or dancing, in church services or in general. While this rule is

crumbling, it remains a point of controversy among strongly religious American Christians. This has mostly not been the case for African-American churches, whose services have historically been strongly, rhythmically oriented. What is the history here? I've seen some Christians say that while the Bible mentions several musical instruments being used in a worship context, drums are not among them. Is that the whole story? Or is the racist subtext of this rule the real story?

**A.** There are several Old Testament texts where drums were used and worshiping God was a very joyous exciting event. The Ancients would dance mightily before the Lord and music was a very important part of their services. David wrote many of the psalms and had them sent to his Chief Musician to be used and taught to the People. God used music as a means to teach His word and for prophesy. Ezekiel for example, was a prophet that would sing and all the people would hear him and speak well of his voice. Unfortunately they also ignored the messages in his words.

> And they come unto thee as the people cometh, and they sit before thee *as* my people, and they hear thy words, but they will not do them: for with their mouth they shew much love, *but* their heart goeth after their covetousness. And, lo, thou *art* unto them as a very lovely song of one that hath a pleasant voice, and can play well on an instrument: for they hear thy words, but they do them not (Ezekiel 33:31-32).

There were several types of instrument used and most likely, they were portable, stringed instrument, horns and a tambourine like instrument they called a **timbrelH8608** so it is not likely they had huge organs that some Churches use today.

## H8608

תָּפַף

tâphaph

*taw-faf'*

A primitive root; to *drum*, that is, play (as) on the tambourine: - taber, play with timbrels.

One Passage of scripture describes playing this instrument as the sound of the voice of a dove.

> And Huzzab shall be led away captive, she shall be brought up, and her maids shall lead *her* as with the voice of doves, tabering upon their breasts (Nahum 2:7).

For some reason around 1906, a movement called "The Church of Christ," began thinking that anything from the Old Testament was obsolete. Since no mention of any musical instruments or dancing was being used in any church in the New Testament, they considered them as evil and even ascribing it as satanic. Some of these churches still teach this and so the only music allowed is a cappella singing. This has no biblical foundation however, and is just another tradition of man. Sadly, this has caused many people to look more to the world for entertainment, rather than recognizing the gifts and talents that God has given people and to use those talents to praise God.

Around that same time the Azusa revival began, interestingly, it was started by a black man. Other men of God also began awakening.

A worldwide revival began which is still being felt today. Some of the leaders of these revivals were Smith Wigglesworth, John G. Lake, and Billy Sunday among others. This revival was very wide spread, breaking out spontaneously all over the world. Well established

Churches that were steeped in so much tradition that they could not recognize a move of God, began acting much like the Pharisee's of Jesus day. Rather than repenting they tried to reform and began pushing a legalistic agenda and pointing an accusing finger at the revivalist movements calling them false prophets and teachers under a spirit of delusion.

~~~

**Q.** Is it ok to work on the Sabbath?

But the Sabbath was made to benefit man, and not man to benefit the Sabbath (Mark 2:27).

**A.** The Sabbath; God gives us a day of rest and what do we do? We pollute it. We make the Sabbath Day a point of contention and strife over what we can or cannot do. Jesus said He was Lord of the Sabbath too (Mark 2:28). He also called out, "Come unto me, all ye that labour and are heavy laden, and I will give you rest. Take my yoke upon you, and learn of me; for I am meek and lowly in heart: and ye shall find rest unto your souls. For my yoke is easy, and my burden is light" (Matthew 11:28-30).

I entered into the Lord's Sabbath some time ago when I finally realized that it came down to putting all my care upon Him, because He cares for me (1Peter 5:7). I have also found that once I give the problem to the Lord, I need to leave it with Him. If I pick it back up and try to fix things on my own then I pollute His Sabbath.

The point is the Lord does not want us living as if we are carrying the weight of the world on our shoulders. That is why the scripture tells us to count it all joy when we face problems while we are simply doing the labors that God has for us. As believers, we can be confident that despite whatever problems we are facing our God can handle it. However, to get to this place you must spend time with Jesus. This form of confidence comes from spending time reading, studying, meditating, and sometimes fasting but most important is talking to the Lord, as a dear friend, getting to know Him personally.

The great thing is we can do that anytime. If you do, you will be at perfect peace and you will not concern yourself with working on the Sabbath, because in His peace there is rest. The Sabbath therefore is not a day in time, but a state of being. Yes, you should take a day off to rest your body, but it should not matter which day once you have entered into the Sabbath the Lord provides for you.

~~~

**Q.** I've heard the phrase "God between the gaps." If God exists but doesn't interfere with the Natural World, could He still be meaningful to humans in any practical way? If so; how?

**A.** Yes, as a Christian I believe God can interfere with demonic spiritual activity, in such away as not to leave any evidence of His existence. Moreover, the Bible says, "we know that all things work together for good to them that love God, to them who are the called according to *his* purpose" (Romans 8:28).

I wonder, would you consider God sharing some important information with a believer, or instructing them to do something as interference?

For example if He caused me to walk down a certain street so that my presence scared off an abductor, thus preventing a crime, and saving a child. Or, if He told someone to buy a meal for a family and that random act of kindness, changed their whole attitude about life, and caused them to make changes? Would that be interfering in the natural world?

Sometimes God does things just like that. Nevertheless, most people shrug it off as coincidence.

~~~

**Q.** Does God save people who are not Christians?

    a.  Does God work through what is true and good in non-Christian religions or even atheistic philosophies?

    b.  Can we believe that God wills the salvation of all people and still claim Jesus as the only savior?

**A.** Of course He does, but once you are saved you are no longer a non-Christian. To be a Christian you have to be reborn as one. A person is born into the world by natural childbirth. When they become old enough to know right from wrong, they need to receive Christ as their lord and believe in their heart that God raised Him from death to life. This causes a miracle of a new birth and a non-Christian becomes a New Creation in Christ, and yes, you are *saved* with all the benefits of being a child of God, and have eternal life.

    **a.**  Does God work through what is true and good in non-Christian religions or even atheistic philosophies?

    **A.**  Yes, He does, but just because God works through someone that is not a Christian, does not mean they will automatically become one. The choice to believe in Christ and His gospel still belongs to you, so essentially you are responsible for your own salvation.

    **b.**  Can we believe that God wills the salvation of all people and still claim Jesus as the only savior?

    **A.**  You have just shown exactly how God feels about the matter. The bible says that, "The Lord is not slack concerning his promise, as some men count slackness; but is longsuffering to us-ward, not willing that any should perish, but that all should come to repentance." (2Peter 3:9) You see God wants everybody to be saved and He made a way to be saved through Jesus Christ. He has poured out His Spirit on everyone and is standing at the door of their Heart asking to come in so He can have fellowship with them (Revelation 3:20).

~~~

**Q.** If Christian Catechism is true in stating that God created man to, "know Him, love Him and serve Him" then why does a perfect being need to be loved and served?

**A.** He does not so much need us to serve Him, however; He seems to take great pleasure in serving us. The first thing God did after He sent Adam and Eve out of the Garden was bless them. That word literally means to kneel and serve.

However, to deal with the Love part of your question, it is again His Love towards us that keeps Him from just obliterating all of humanity. If you have ever loved someone like your children then you will understand that as much as you love them and want what is best for them, you must also allow them to grow and make their own way in the world. You hope that they will do well and show the world a few of the things you have given them, in the many interactions you had raising them. If you did a reasonably decent job in that then you have a certain pride in them.

God is sort of like that. He loves all of us, but still it is up to us whether or not we accept Him, or rebel against Him.

~~~

**Q.** Why don't Christian women cover their head?

1 Corinthians 11:5-6 "But every woman who prays or prophesies with her head uncovered dishonors her head—it is the same as having her head shaved. For if a woman does not cover her head, she might as well have her hair cut off"~ NIV

I am just wondering what the Christian view of this is; is it completely ignored? If the Bible is believed to be the word of God (divinely inspired) I would read the above as an instruction from God to all believing woman to cover their head, yet the only ones I see covering their head these days are not Christian. Looking at old pictures from 100 years ago, I can see that head covering was more common in Britain for example but that is not the case now. Are there no honorable Christian women left in this day and age?

**A.** If you take that in full context then it goes on to say that the head of the woman is the man and the covering of the man is Christ. This is telling Christian women to pray for their husbands. Since the head of the man is Christ, the man's Head (Jesus) does not need covering.

Because of persecutions, Paul wrote in such a way that unbelievers could not understand the higher Spiritual meaning behind the words. During the dark ages, much of that Spiritual revelation was lost to traditions and for several centuries, Christian women took the words literally, and wore very fine hats. It made a being a hatter, a very good business, but really did not bring them any closer to the knowledge of God or make any impression on God, as to whether or not He would answer their prayers.

What I get most from the passage is that God's angels are watching families. When they live with a respect for each other and humbly before Christ then those angels stand at the ready to perform the requests made during prayer or to operate on the prophetic words she may speak.

~~~

**Q.** How can you know that you are saved?

**A.** Romans 10:6-13 says that,

> The righteousness which is of faith speaketh on this wise, Say not in thine heart, Who shall ascend into heaven? (that is, to bring Christ down *from above:*) Or, Who shall descend into the deep? (that is, to bring up Christ again from the dead.) But what saith it? The word is nigh thee, *even* in thy mouth, and in thy heart: that is, the word of faith, which we preach;

> That if thou shalt confess with thy mouth the Lord Jesus, and shalt believe in thine heart that God hath raised him from the dead, thou shalt be saved. For with the heart man believeth unto righteousness; and with the mouth confession is made unto salvation. For the scripture saith, Whosoever believeth on him shall not be ashamed. For there is no difference between the Jew and the Greek: for the same Lord over all is rich unto all that call upon him. For whosoever shall call upon the name of the Lord shall be saved." This scripture is a clear and concise promise of God's plan of salvation.

~~~

**Q.** Has there ever been any discussion amongst the leaders of the major Christian denominations about merging?

**A.** I don't think the leaders have ever gotten together and discussed it, but I think many leaders think all the other denominations should abandon their beliefs, and join them. A few leaders have switched denominations and even tried to bring some of their colleagues with them.

The thing is it really isn't within the power of man to unify the Church. Eventually the Holy Spirit will begin to unify us, but for now I think the diversity of denominations, is sort of advantageous to reach an even more diverse world. I think that the Churches are getting better at recognizing the legitimacy of each ones role in the Body of Christ even if we still do not know what each ones position is in the body. The following verses talk about the complexity of the body of Christ.

> There should be no schism in the body; but that the members should have the same care one for another. And whether one member suffer, all the members suffer with it; or one member be honoured, all the members rejoice with it. Now ye are the body of Christ, and members in particular (1Corenthians 12:25-27).

> For the body is not one member, but many. If the foot shall say, Because I am not the hand, I am not of the body; is it therefore not of the body? And if the ear shall say, Because I am not the eye, I am not of the body; is it therefore not of the body? If the whole body were an eye, where were the hearing? If the whole were hearing, where were the smelling? But now hath God set the members every one of them in the body, as it hath pleased him. And if they were all one member, where were the body? But now are they many members, yet but one body. And the eye cannot say unto the hand, I have no need of thee: nor again the head to the feet, I have no need of you (1Corenthians 12:14-21).

> For I say, through the grace given unto me, to every man that is among you, not to think of himself more highly than he ought to think; but to think soberly, according as God hath dealt to every man the measure of faith. For as we have many members in one body, and all members have not the same office:

> So we, being many, are one body in Christ, and every one members one of another. Having then gifts differing according to the grace that is given to us, whether prophecy, let us prophesy according to the proportion of faith; Or ministry, let us wait on our ministering: or he that teacheth, on teaching; Or he that exhorteth, on exhortation: he that giveth, let him do it with simplicity; he that ruleth, with diligence; he that sheweth mercy, with cheerfulness (Romans 12:3-8).

When all the denominations begin to realize that those things go beyond the denomination, then it will not be long before the body of Christ is fully formed. Then we will finally represent Christ in the Earth, as a glorious church, without spot blemish or wrinkle. We are not there yet.

〜〜〜

**Q.** According to the bible, is it a sin for men to have long hair?

> 1Corinthians 11:14 says it's shameful. But Samson had long hair.

**A.** No, in fact in the Old Testament God calls for certain men, such as Samson, to be Nazarites and says that if a person should take the vow of a Nazarite they should consecrate themselves which included allowing hair to grow.

> And the LORD spake unto Moses, saying, Speak unto the children of Israel, and say unto them, When either man or woman shall separate themselves to vow a vow of a Nazarite, to separate themselves unto the LORD:
>
> He shall separate himself from wine and strong drink, and shall drink no vinegar of wine, or vinegar of strong drink, neither shall he drink any liquor of grapes, nor eat moist grapes, or dried. All the days of his separation shall he eat nothing that is made of the vine tree, from the kernels even to the husk.
>
> All the days of the vow of his separation there shall no razor come upon his head: until the days be fulfilled, in the which he separateth himself unto the LORD, he shall be holy, and shall let the locks of the hair of his head grow (Numbers 6:1-5).

Notice that either a man or a woman could be a Nazarite by choice. However this is not a New Testament doctrine, but came under the Law of Moses. The New Testament teachings that speak about a man's hair being long are...

> Doth not even nature itself teach you, that, if a man have long hair, it is a shame unto him? But if a woman have long hair, it is a glory to her: for *her* hair is given her for a covering. But if any man seem to be contentious, we have no such custom, neither the churches of God (1Corinthians 11:14-16).

Paul was using a local custom, to teach a far greater truth. The eleventh chapter of 1stCorinthians deals with a biblical marriage. Christ is the Head of the husband and the husband is the head of the wife. He is using what should appear to be a natural truth, to teach a Spiritual reality. He clearly stated in verse 16 that there is no custom concerning hair length in the Churches of God, for either a man or a woman. It also seems clear to me that Paul did not want any arguments springing up about hair length.

~~~

**Q.** Why are you a Christian?

**A.** I am a Christian because most of my life was spent trying to please God and doing the right thing. I found it impossible and gave up; I started trying to live to make me happy, that too became impossible. So I turned to exploring other religions and I found such diversity that they could not all be correct. Furthermore, I saw no means to try to reconcile them into one universal truth.

I found myself more and more confused but not willing to concede that life just sprang from lifelessness nor that such a complex and diverse universe could happen by chance. Finally, I called out to whatever God is real. That He would have to show me the right path to truth, because no matter how intelligent I thought I was, I could not figure it out. I declared that, "If I wound up in hell it would be His fault because at this very moment I am putting my salvation on Him." If He wanted to save me, He had to do it. I was too weak and to ignorant.

I picked up a bible and began reading it and God began teaching right from the pages of His word. As I looked back over my life, I realized He had been with me my whole life orchestrating things to show me my limitations and need for His salvation. He filled me with His Spirit, and the scriptures really began to open up to me. He taught me things that I could never have seen or understood. Things beyond hermeneutics, or what pastors had told me.

Soon after I had prayed, He led me to a church and in one night Pastor Beechard Moorefield, confirmed everything the Lord had shown me. He then set me in that church, so I could grow. For years after I would read my bible and Pastor Moorefield would confirm everything God had shown me. It was as if I knew what he would preach about, before I sat down.

~~~

**Q.** What is God to you?

**A.** God is not a "what." He is a person, He speaks to me, reassures me, brings people into my life; some to say "Don't get ahead of yourself" and some to say "you got this." He is a Father, a provider, and a Friend that sticks closer than a brother.

He causes me to remember Him, and gives a greater meaning to my life. He opens doors that no one else can and closes doors so no one can reopen them. He is a personal God. He is not in some box limited to my idea of Him, because He promises great things are still to come, and with Him nothing is impossible.

He forgives me when I fail, picks me up and sets me back on the path. He is everything in the Psalm 23 and Psalm 91. He has a purpose for my life and so I go about sharing His gospel. Anyone who will listen can meet him, because He is able to do all that for me and for you if you will allow Him. He is never too busy to talk to you.

~~~

**Q.** Does God give preferential treatment to people who believe in His existence? If so; why?

**A.** There are a lot of people who say they believe in God, even in the Christian God, but God says "without faith it is impossible to please him: for he that cometh to God must believe that he is, and that he is a rewarder of them that diligently seek him" (Hebrews 11:6).

The bible also teaches that a faith of simply believing in His existence is not sufficient to garner God's preferential attention.

> So speak ye, and so do, as they that shall be judged by the law of liberty. For he shall have judgment without mercy, that hath shewed no mercy; and mercy rejoiceth against judgment. 14 What doth it profit, my brethren, though a man say he hath faith, and have not works? can faith save him?
>
> If a brother or sister be naked, and destitute of daily food, And one of you say unto them, Depart in peace, be ye warmed and filled; notwithstanding ye give them not those things which are needful to the body; what doth it profit? Even so faith, if it hath not works, is dead, being alone.
>
> Yea, a man may say, Thou hast faith, and I have works: shew me thy faith without thy works, and I will shew thee my faith by my works. Thou believest that there is one God; thou doest well: the devils also believe, and tremble. But wilt thou know, O vain man, that faith without works is dead? (James 2:12-20).

What James is saying is that because of real faith, a person will willingly give things that are necessary for life to people in need.

Moreover, because he is giving in Faith, he can expect God to reward him in both this life and the next. If that is not preferential treatment then I do not know what is. However, the answer to your question is "NO," not for just believing in His existence.

This aligns with both the Old and New Testaments, Jesus himself said that God gives good gifts to those that ask Him.

> If ye then, being evil, know how to give good gifts unto your children, how much more shall your Father which is in heaven give good things to them that ask him? (Mathew 7:11).

> If ye then, being evil, know how to give good gifts unto your children: how much more shall *your* heavenly Father give the Holy Spirit to them that ask him? (Luke 11:13).

Nevertheless, He also said that you could not come to the Father except through Him and no one comes to Jesus except the Father reveals it to them.

> All that the Father giveth me shall come to me; and him that cometh to me I will in no wise cast out (John 6:37).

> Jesus saith unto him, I am the way, the truth, and the life: no man cometh unto the Father, but by me (John 14:6).

In other words, God does give preferential treatment to His children and you cannot be a child of God unless you believe in Jesus.

~~~

**Q.** What would you consider to be your life verse(s)" or "life scripture(s)" and why?

**A.** Oddly enough it is Deuteronomy 8:18 "But thou shalt remember the LORD thy God: for it is he that giveth thee power to get wealth, that he may establish his covenant which he sware unto thy fathers, as it is this day."

This is the scripture that the Lord used to call me into ministry although it took me some time to comprehend its meaning.

There are three factions to this verse:

For most people, the first part sounds like a commandment "But thou shalt remember the LORD thy God." But the Lord showed me this is his greatest promise to me. He taught me it means he will remind me that He is. The onus of remembering Him is not on me. In the Old Testament the people the Lord spoke to was not able to be reborn, the Holy Spirit could not be poured out upon all flesh so for them it was more of a commandment. The onus to remember God fell to the ability of men. I used to be afraid of this verse, I felt that if I prospered I would do what he warned against in Deuteronomy 8:19, "And it shall be, if thou do at all forget the LORD thy God, and walk after other gods, and serve them, and worship them, I testify against you this day that ye shall surely perish." I became afraid to prosper, because I thought I would get caught up in the deceitfulness of riches and lose sight of God, lose my salvation, and I felt paralyzed. In truth I was paralyzed, useless to God and myself. God freed me because the onus of remembering Him is on Him. So how does He keep me reminded of Him? The first four words say a lot, "But, thou shalt remember." It was God telling me I would remember because He said I would remember. The only thing I needed to do was believe it. The onus of remembering was lifted from my natural mind and switched to the onus of faith; God pleasing faith. God pleasing faith is acting on what God tells you. From there He taught me that all I have is His and is to be used for His covenant. I cannot tell you how much this freed me and delivered me from fearing that I would become greedy or trust in worldly possessions. Think about it what appeared to be a commandment and a burden Jesus made into a promise... WOW!

Secondly, you see it no longer matters to me if my bank account has thousands of dollars, or ten dollars, because it is not my money. If I live in a mud hut or a mansion, "For it is he that giveth thee power to get wealth." God will watch over me, he is my dwelling place and my Shepherd. He is with me always and whatever I do, he still loves me and is my constant companion. The power of God is within me to get the wealth to meet all of needs and to be a blessing to others. In fact the power of God is in me to get the "True Riches," with which I will bless entire nations. Some people may say I am thinking too highly of myself, but I am convinced that this is Gods will for all believers. Jesus said, "If we cannot be trusted with the unrighteous mammon, who would trust us with the 'true riches.'" What are the true riches? Among them are wisdom, peace, joy, and yes the power to get wealth, the power to get your needs met and be a blessing to others.

Finally, because whatever the lord places under my stewardship whether great or small it is given, "That he may establish his covenant which he sware unto thy fathers, as it is this day." Even though I sometimes fail by giving to unfruitful works, I know I can go to him and ask for forgiveness. I am learning to be a wiser steward and I am promised true riches which have eternal value.

~~~

**Q.** What are your core beliefs as a Christian?

Concerning Judgment, Giving, Tithing, Worship, etc. I believe that God will someday bring all Christians to a unity of the Faith according to Ephesians 4:13. I thought I would give my fellow Christians an opportunity to share what you believe all Christians should believe.

**A.** I believe that there is one God who exists as three distinct persons which, we can relate to as The Father, Jesus the Son and The Holy Spirit. He is the creator of all that is. I believe that He came to Earth in the person of Jesus, the Messiah, in the form of the Son of God. He was born of a virgin, and showed us by example His righteousness and authority. He is all-powerful and is unchanging yet willfully allowed himself to be tortured and killed, so that He could conquer the power of sin and death for all men.

I believe that the Bible is the authoritative Word of God, that brings people to Christ, through the Gospel of the Lordship of Jesus. So that whosoever believes in Him, and that God raised Him from the dead, shall be saved. I believe that God is perfect love and it is His love for us that caused Him to send Jesus, to seek for us and save us from our fallen state.

~What is man, that thou art mindful of him? ~
(Hebrews 2:6)

I believe that God made man in His image and at the deepest part of man, we are good.

Thou madest him a little lower than the angels; thou crownedst him with glory and honour, and didst set him over the works of thy hands: Thou hast put all

> things in subjection under his feet. For in that he put
> all in subjection under him, he left nothing that is not
> put under him. But now we see not yet all things put
> under him. (Hebrews 2:7-8)

Sin has taken humanity captive, and brought death, and suffering. We are fallen from the glory, which God intended us to have. The things intended to be in subjection to us now rebel against us.

I believe that the whole of creation is in travail, and waiting for the sons of God to unify into the perfect stature of Christ. I believe that for this to happen we need to learn to listen to the Holy Spirit, who leads us into all truth. I believe that in order to bring us to that unified Body of Christ, we will be given a Devine Revelation, which will be confirmed by prophets and evangelists worldwide.

> Surely the Lord GOD will do nothing, but he revealeth
> his secret unto his servants the prophets. The lion hath
> roared, who will not fear? the Lord GOD hath spoken,
> who can but prophesy? (Amos 3:7-8)

I believe that there will be a great revival before the tribulation period. The word of God will again be preached with the same authority as was given the early apostles throughout the whole world as a final witness against it. When everyone has been given an opportunity to accept Jesus then all those who do will be raptured out. Once the Glorious Church is removed, there will be nothing to prevent the antichrist from coming into power. Those who are left behind will be forced to choose between worshiping the beast, or going into hiding. There will be two witnesses sent to cause problems for the beast and they will preach the gospel, and help those who are left behind until they are martyred. When there are no more people left on Earth who will call upon the name of the Lord, then the wrath of God will be poured out and the end will come.

~~~

**Q.** Why do so many theists care what atheists believe?

I'm puzzled by this. Is it a hobby? Is it simply trolling for giggles? If you are a Christian, Muslim or Hindu, can you please tell me why it matters to you what I or anyone else has for a personal belief system?

**A.** As a Christian, I have an obligation to spread the Gospel but that in and of itself pales to the love I receive and that flows through me when I do. I have also found that I am capable of loving strangers and people I have never met. I have been convicted to pray for people in all sorts of circumstances, the poor, the rich, atheists, politicians celebrities; you see we all need the Lord.

I can only speak for myself, and I do care about your soul's salvation. I do not believe it serves God in the least to sit and debate our beliefs but I do believe in sharing mine as long as you are willing to listen. I am not a trained apologist or a theologian, 75% of what I know from scriptures comes from my personal study, meditation and prayer. The rest came from my teacher/pastor. Ultimately, all truth comes from the Lord. Do not get me wrong, I am quite sure that some of my beliefs are error and there is still much I have yet to learn.

~~~

**Q.** Why are Christians concerned so much about what Jesus talked about the least in the bible?

Christians are concerned so much about homosexuality, sexual sin and so forth, but those subjects that are covered the least in the New Testament—but, care nothing about condemning, lying, "talking behind backs" and so forth.

**A.** Most seasoned Christians are not as concerned about those things; people looking to stir up controversy put it out there to create confusion. Those of us, who have spent time with the Lord, know He is not pleased about many things. But it is not our job to force unbelievers to obey God. The most we can do is plant seeds and pray. It is the Holy Spirits job to prick the hearts of nonbelievers regardless of our personal feelings about people and their life choices.

~~~

**Q.** How is a person saved (know they are going to heaven)?

**A.** The righteousness which is of faith speaketh on this wise, Say not in thine heart, Who shall ascend into heaven? (that is, to bring Christ down *from above:*) Or, Who shall descend into the deep? (that is, to bring up Christ again from the dead.) But what saith it? The word is nigh thee, *even* in thy mouth, and in thy heart: that is, the word of faith, which we preach;

> That if thou shalt confess with thy mouth the Lord Jesus, and shalt believe in thine heart that God hath raised him from the dead, thou shalt be saved. For with the heart man believeth unto righteousness; and with the mouth confession is made unto salvation. For the scripture saith, Whosoever believeth on him shall not be ashamed.

> For there is no difference between the Jew and the
> Greek: for the same Lord over all is rich unto all that
> call upon him.
>
> For whosoever shall call upon the name of the Lord
> shall be saved (Rom 10:6-13).

There you have a very straightforward answer right from the Word of God.

**Q.** Will the meek truly inherit the Earth?

Just seems unlikely to me. (Matthew 5:5) Why do the meek deserve it so much?

**A.** For one to be meek is to choose to submit to authority. In the case of, "Blessed are the meek: for they shall inherit the earth," (Mathew 5:5) it would mean quite simply to choose to follow the will of God.

God does not force anyone to follow Him, but has given us all free will to choose that path. I should say here that meekness is not a prerequisite to salvation, but is quite often a manifestation of it. A willingness to give up your ways and seek after God's way as Christ did.

> Then said Jesus unto them, When ye have lifted up
> the Son of man, then shall ye know that I am *he,* and
> *that* I do nothing of myself; but as my Father hath
> taught me, I speak these things. And he that sent me
> is with me: the Father hath not left me alone; for I do
> always those things that please him. (John 8:28-29).

This is our guide for meekness. It may seem difficult or strange but the eventual reward for this obedience is to inherit the Earth.

However, in practical matters a person who submits their free will/ authority to someone other than Christ is likely only going to inherit emptiness and loss. Even when thinking they have gained the trust of someone in a position to promote them, they will find they are being used in their new position. Remember your life is worth more than any Earthly gain.

~~~

# Chapter 5

## Jesus

*"Jesus is hungry but feeds others; He grows weary but offers others rest; He is the King Messiah but pays tribute; He is called the devil but casts out demons; He dies the death of a sinner but comes to save His people from their sins; He is sold for thirty pieces of silver but gives His life a ransom for many; He will not turn stones to bread for Himself but gives His own body as bread for people." D.A. Carson*

*"When we have accepted Jesus Christ, we have become akin to the Father; having become real children of God, we then have the spirit of sonship by which we can come into His presence and make known our wants in a familiar way." A.C. Dixon*

1.  If Jesus Christ is the biological son of God, why does the Bible list His genealogy through His stepfather Joseph?
2.  Where did the *Christ* surname originate? Was that Mary's name?
3.  Why did Jesus curse a fig tree?
4.  How would Jesus criticize some Christian leaders today?
5.  Did Jesus like bananas?
6.  Did Jesus Christ really know what it was like to be human?
7.  Why did Jesus say whoever loves his/her father, mother, spouse, children and etc. cannot be His follower?
8.  Is Jesus' personality unique enough?
9.  Are the things about Jesus Christ actually true?
    Did Jesus have any brothers or sisters? Did Mary have any children with Joseph?

**Q.** If Jesus Christ is the biological son of God, why does the Bible list His genealogy through His stepfather Joseph?

**A.** As strange as this may sound, even though Joseph was not the biological father of Jesus, when he married Mary they became one flesh and Jesus was in her womb at the time. This fulfilled the Scripture that Jesus would be born to a descendant of King David

~~~

**Q.** Where did the *Christ* surname originate? Was that Mary's name?

**A.** Christ is not a surname and no, it is not Mary or Joseph's name. The term *Christ* comes from the Greek word *Chirstos* and was used by early Jewish translators when writing the gospels whenever associating Jesus as the anointed one or Messiah. The following shows the relationship between the words "messiah" and "christ."

> Andrew first findeth his own brother Simon, and saith unto him, We have found the Messias, which is, being interpreted, the Christ (John 1:41).

This came from Daniel's prophesy,

> Know therefore and understand, *that* from the going forth of the commandment to restore and to build Jerusalem unto the Messiah the Prince *shall be* seven weeks, and threescore and two weeks: the street shall be built again, and the wall, even in troublous times. And after threescore and two weeks shall Messiah be cut off, but not for himself: and the people of the prince that shall come shall destroy the city and the sanctuary; and the end thereof *shall be* with a flood, and unto the end of the war desolations are determined (Daniel 9:25-26).

Using the Strong's Concordance and Lexicons, we can trace the etymology *(origins and developments)* of both words.

G5547
Χριστός
Christos
khris-tos'
From G5548; anointed, that is, the Messiah, an epithet of Jesus: - Christ.

G5548
χρίω
chrio‾
khree'-o
Probably akin to G5530 through the idea of contact; to smear or rub with oil, that is, (by implication) to consecrate to an office or religious service: - anoint.

G3323
Μεσσίας
Messias
*mes-see'-as*
Of Hebrew origin [H4899]; the *Messias* (that is, *Mashiach*), or Christ: - Messias.

**H4899**
משׁיח
mâshîyach
*maw-shee'-akh*
From **H4886**; *anointed*; usually a *consecrated* person (as a king, priest, or saint); specifically the *Messiah:* - anointed, Messiah.

## H4886

מָשַׁח

mâshach

*maw-shakh'*

A primitive root; to *rub* with oil, that is, to *anoint*; by implication to *consecrate*; also to *paint:* - anoint, paint. (Strong's Greek and Hebrew Lexicons)

The word *Christ* grew out of an ancient Hebrew ceremony of anointing or rubbing down certain men with a special cocktail of spices and fragrant oils that, once completed, set the individual apart for certain Jewish positions in their culture—usually to become a prophet, priest or king. There is no record of Jesus being anointed with oil and spices until a certain woman came on one occasion and Mary came on another occasion and anointed His feet, (Luke 7:38, John 12:3)

The Holy Spirit anointed Jesus on the day John the Baptist baptized Him. "And Jesus, when he was baptized, went up straightway out of the water: and, lo, the heavens were opened unto him, and he saw the Spirit of God descending like a dove, and lighting upon him" (Mathew 3:16). Afterwards Jesus went into the desert for forty days. When He returned He began preaching everywhere and when He reached His hometown this is what happened,

> And he came to Nazareth, where he had been brought up: and, as his custom was, he went into the synagogue on the sabbath day, and stood up for to read. And there was delivered unto him the book of the prophet Esaias. And when he had opened the book, he found the place where it was written,

> The Spirit of the Lord is upon me, because he hath anointed me to preach the gospel to the poor; he hath sent me to heal the brokenhearted, to preach

deliverance to the captives, and recovering of sight to the blind, to set at liberty them that are bruised, To preach the acceptable year of the Lord.

And he closed the book, and he gave it again to the minister, and sat down. And the eyes of all them that were in the synagogue were fastened on him. And he began to say unto them, This day is this scripture fulfilled in your ears. (Luke 4:16-21)

His words and actions said, "I am the Christ or Messiah."

~~~

**Q.** Why did Jesus curse a fig tree?

The situation involving the cursed fig tree is recorded in two places in the gospels— Matthew 21:18-22 and Mark 11:12-14; 20-25. Several things about this are hard to understand. Why Jesus with His extreme goodness would curse a tree created by God to die? Similarly why would Jesus cause the death of a large number of pigs (Mark5:10)? It does not look like something Jesus would do.

**A.** I like Mark's version of the fig tree story,

And on the morrow, when they were come from Bethany, he was hungry: And seeing a fig tree afar off having leaves, he came, if haply he might find any thing thereon: and when he came to it, he found nothing but leaves; for the time of figs was not yet.

And Jesus answered and said unto it, No man eat fruit of thee hereafter for ever. And his disciples heard it. (Mark 11:12-14)

Jesus demonstrated what happens to hypocrites who try to pass themselves off as fruit bearers when they do not really produce anything but draw a lot of attention to themselves. The fig tree was "seen from afar off" it looked as if it should be full of figs. It is representative of the Pharisees' doctrines that attracted a lot of people but did not feed them. Another thing we see is that "the time of figs was not yet." This signifies false prophets/christs who seem as if they know something but come before the time.

As for the Swine or pigs,

> And they came over unto the other side of the sea, into the country of the Gadarenes. And when he was come out of the ship, immediately there met him out of the tombs a man with an unclean spirit, Who had his dwelling among the tombs; and no man could bind him, no, not with chains: Because that he had been often bound with fetters and chains, and the chains had been plucked asunder by him, and the fetters broken in pieces: neither could any man tame him. And always, night and day, he was in the mountains, and in the tombs, crying, and cutting himself with stones.

> But when he saw Jesus afar off, he ran and worshipped him, And cried with a loud voice, and said, What have I to do with thee, Jesus, thou Son of the most high God? I adjure thee by God, that thou torment me not.

> For he said unto him, Come out of the man, thou unclean spirit.

> And he asked him, What is thy name? And he answered, saying, My name is Legion: for we are

> many. And he besought him much that he would not
> send them away out of the country.
>
> Now there was there nigh unto the mountains a great
> herd of swine feeding. And all the devils besought
> him, saying, Send us into the swine, that we may
> enter into them. And forthwith Jesus gave them leave.
> And the unclean spirits went out, and entered into the
> swine: and the herd ran violently down a steep place
> into the sea, (they were about two thousand;) and
> were choked in the sea. (Mark 5:1–13)

Jesus permitted the demons to enter swine because He did not want a whole legion of demons loose on the town. Swine are forbidden to the Jews because they do not chew the cud even though they have cloven hoofs, "And the swine, because it divideth the hoof, yet cheweth not the cud, it is unclean unto you: ye shall not eat of their flesh, nor touch their dead carcase" (Deuteronomy 14:8). This represents religious leaders who look holy. In a sense, they follow their religion (hence the cloven hoof) but they do not meditate and pray over the Word of God (chew the cud) which produces solid teaching to feed their followers. If they did, it would eventually become revelation knowledge of God's word "strong meat." The "dead carcase" is symbolic of dead works; which is saying do not become involved in religious or charity work that does not teach sound biblical doctrines and is not involved in spreading the gospel.

Demons are walking about to see whom they can devour (1Peter 5:8). Allowing them to enter the swine kept them from entering into people. Also, people who are very religious but reject Christ and the Gospel are very susceptible to demonic possession. However, the promise of Jesus is that all those who believe in Him and ask the Father can receive the gift of the Holy Ghost.

If ye then, being evil, know how to give good gifts unto your children: how much more shall your heavenly Father give the Holy Spirit to them that ask him? (Luke 11:13)

Follow Godly men and, "as newborn babes, desire the sincere milk of the word, that ye may grow thereby:" (1Peter 2:2). "For when for the time ye ought to be teachers, ye have need that one teach you again which be the first principles of the oracles of God; and are become such as have need of milk, and not of strong meat. For every one that useth milk is unskilful in the word of righteousness: for he is a babe. But strong meat belongeth to them that are of full age, even those who by reason of use have their senses exercised to discern both good and evil:" (Hebrews 5:12-14).

~~~

**Q.** How would Jesus criticize some Christian leaders today?

**A.** Whenever Jesus said, "woe" it had a prophetic purpose behind it. Everything He needed to say about religion is written in the gospels of the Holy Bible. Religion has not really changed much; it has its followers and its hypocrites. Neither one would likely please Him. Still He is merciful in His displeasure but more importantly, He is gracious to those who have managed to get it right. The gospel of the Kingdom of God is not a script filled with rules of, "do this; don't do that." Rather, it is a message of peace and fellowship between the believer and God the creator.

~~~

**Q.** Did Jesus like bananas?

**A.** I am sure He does enjoy bananas and all sorts of foods that were not available in that region during the days when He walked the Earth. Every time they are offered in kindness to the hungry.

> For I was an hungred, and ye gave me meat: I was thirsty, and ye gave me drink: I was a stranger, and ye took me in: Naked, and ye clothed me: I was sick, and ye visited me: I was in prison, and ye came unto me.

> Then shall the righteous answer him, saying, Lord, when saw we thee an hungred, and fed *thee?* or thirsty, and gave *thee* drink? When saw we thee a stranger, and took *thee* in? or naked, and clothed *thee?* Or when saw we thee sick, or in prison, and came unto thee?

> And the King shall answer and say unto them, Verily I say unto you, Inasmuch as ye have done *it* unto one of the least of these my brethren, ye have done *it* unto me.(Mathew 25:35-40)

I suppose even bananas would qualify here.

~~~

**Q.** Did Jesus Christ really know what it was like to be human?

1.  He never sinned - no other person has been able to do this, so it's obvious that there was something un-human about him.
2.  He went 40 days without food or water - in the desert. No human can go more than a few days without water.
3.  He never had a sexual relationship with a woman.

    Considering this, how could He have the slightest idea what it is like to be human?

**A.** The Bible says, "For we have not an high priest which cannot be touched with the feeling of our infirmities; but was in all points tempted like as *we are, yet* without sin" (Hebrew 4:15).

He never had sex but a woman tempted Him when she, caught in an adulteress act, was brought to Him (John 8:3-11.) This is a very famous story but what many people miss is that they caught her in the act. Jesus does not look on her but turns and writes in the ground to avoid being drawn into the temptation.

He was tempted with hunger by the devil during those 40 days without food "And the devil said unto him, If thou be the Son of God, command this stone that it be made bread" (Luke 4:3). It never says He went that long without water.

He was indeed without sin but being human is not about committing sin. Jesus knows that we will sin. His sinless life was possible because even though He was a man, He was still God. As the Messiah, the Word of God concerning Him by the ancient prophets was what kept Him from sin. Especially this verse, "For he shall give his angels charge over thee, to keep thee in all thy ways" (Psalm 91:11). That and His ability to communicate and hear from the Father; although He had these temptations He chose to do what the Father told Him to do, "And he that sent me is with me: the Father hath not left me alone; for I do always those things that please him" (John 8:29).

His greatest temptation came just before His death on the cross. He could have called for twelve legions of angels to deliver Him. "Thinkest thou that I cannot now pray to my Father, and he shall presently give me more than twelve legions of angels?" (Mathew 26:53). If He had chosen that path those angels would have delivered Him and destroyed the whole Earth. Instead, He chose to make the ultimate sacrifice for us all. Why? Because He loves us, as it is written, "Greater love hath no man than this, that a man lay down his life for his friends," (John 15:13).

***An anonymous person continued the conversation.***

q.   Did He really die for us? His death was very temporary - only three days. At most, it seems like a minor inconvenience. Where's the sacrifice? If He stayed dead, that would have been a sacrifice.

Do you think He would have offered to die permanently if it would have saved all of humanity?

***My response to them,***

a.   Yes, He died for us. Being without sin He did not have to die, but made the conscience choice to pay our sin debt. His sacrifice should not be minimized. You seem to be having trouble recognizing that Christ is Holy, and His death was unwarranted. He did nothing in which to be put to death for. As I wrote in the original answer, He could have called twelve legions of angels to deliver Him and sent the whole Earth into the lake of fire permanently. Even during His Earthly walk, He was not treated with the honor He deserved, although He constantly sought to see if any had recognized Him for who He truly was.

Jesus knows what He put into humanity and the power He gave us from the beginning. We were designed to be gods and to be His companions. Because we sin, He cannot have that fellowship with us. Moreover, to allow us the ability of the power of a god, with an evil heart, would not work out so well. This is why the punishment seems so wrong to some people. The knowledge and abilities we have are nothing compared to what He wants for us, what He put in us. In this Proverb God is looking for something, He says, "The spirit of man is the candle of the LORD, searching all the inward parts of the belly" (Proverbs 20:27)

What do you think He is looking for?

~~~

**Q.** Why did Jesus say whoever loves his/her father, mother, spouse, children and etc. cannot be His follower?

**A.** Let's look at the entire text;

First in Mathew

> 34 Think not that I am come to send peace on earth: I came not to send peace, but a sword. 35 For I am come to set a man at variance against his father, and the daughter against her mother, and the daughter in law against her mother in law.
>
> 36 And a man's foes shall be they of his own household. 37 He that loveth father or mother more than me is not worthy of me: and he that loveth son or daughter more than me is not worthy of me (Mathew 10:34-37).

Then in Luke

> 26 If any man come to me, and hate not his father, and mother, and wife, and children, and brethren, and sisters, yea, and his own life also, he cannot be my disciple. 27 And whosoever doth not bear his cross, and come after me, cannot be my disciple. 28 For

> which of you, intending to build a tower, sitteth not
> down first, and counteth the cost, whether he have
> sufficient to finish it? (Luke 14:26-28).

Jesus was saying that if you become a disciple, your family may, and often will turn against you. He was not advocating the follower to turn against them, but this is also a work of repentance. Most of what you thought you knew, or accepted as truth, God may very well change. The people you trusted before, you may not trust in anymore. If you listen to what they are saying, you will not hear what Jesus is telling you. However, this is about discipleship not salvation. He does not expect everyone to become a disciple, at least not at that level. Also, if you know the Bible says something but instead of trusting it you go to family for advice, you are not being a true disciple.

Sometimes when a believer starts to grow in knowledge and understanding in the things of God, they will began to feel prompted to do things that the family does not understand. This is even true if the whole family is believers. In Luke, the Lord explains that if you will follow Him you need to count the costs before you do. He understands that His enemy is working against Him and that the minute you try to take that greater step of faith that Satan will stir up problems for you and one of those areas will be strife in your own family.

I have been there, it is no fun, and it cost me dearly, but I have found that my sons have grown up to be good men in their own right. I am divorced now, but I am happier too. My brother and sisters are beginning to seek Christ now too. Therefore, God is wiser, and more faithful to me, than I have been to Him. My Father finally made peace with me and came to respect me before he passed away. I am not sure if he ever truly accepted Jesus into his own heart. My mother always loved me and accepted my choices. She had her own ideas about Christianity but she did believe in Jesus.

I think my ex-in-laws also have respect for me now. All I can say is that the Lord is faithful and keeps His promises.

> 29 And Jesus answered and said, Verily I say unto you, There is no man that hath left house, or brethren, or sisters, or father, or mother, or wife, or children, or lands, for my sake, and the gospel's, 30 But he shall receive an hundredfold now in this time, houses, and brethren, and sisters, and mothers, and children, and lands, with persecutions; and in the world to come eternal life (Mark 10:29-30).

~~~

**Q.** Is Jesus' personality unique enough?

**A.** I never understand why people try and pigeonhole Jesus. He fully encompassed what it is to be human. The reality is none of us do... Adam was the perfect man but his fall led to the downfall of all men making us less than what Adam was from the beginning. Jesus is called the last Adam, made from the seed of a woman shaped in sin and yet perfect. His life on Earth and what we can read in the gospels reflects only part of His personality as seen through the eyes of the author as he relates what God is giving him to write and through the eyes of the readers of the gospels based on our personalities.

Our personalities are shaped in part by our genetics and in part by our life experiences. Jesus personality is shaped by His Father, and is perfect love, which incorporates all known healthy personalities. He is well able to fully understand you and how to approach you.

~~~

**Q.** Are the things about Jesus Christ actually true?

Is he the son of God? Why didn't God himself come, rather than send His son?

**A.** Jesus was God who became a man temporarily giving up His divine rights as God, and assumed the role of the rights of Adam, before he fell. As a man, He showed us the relationship between man and God as He meant it to be, as between a Perfect Father and perfect son.

He became a man, rather than show himself in the fullness of His glory, because the sin in man cannot approach God, without destroying the man. Even when God dwelt in a gold-lined box so He could get close to us, the only people who could approach the Ark of the Covenant were Levites, and they had to first be atoned by the blood of a perfect lamb.

It never ceases to amaze me that people get that backwards thinking that God could somehow be infected by our sin. His plan is to remove the sin and preserve his most prized creation, which He made in His image, and for His good pleasure, that He may take joy in us.

~~~

**Q.** Did Jesus have any brothers or sisters? Did Mary have any children with Joseph?

**A.** Yes, the clearest Biblical text of this is found in Mathew 12:46-50, Mark 3:31-35 and Mark 6:3.

> While he yet talked to the people, behold, *his* mother and his brethren stood without, desiring to speak with him. Then one said unto him, Behold, thy mother

and thy brethren stand without, desiring to speak
with thee.

But he answered and said unto him that told him,
Who is my mother? and who are my brethren? And he
stretched forth his hand toward his disciples, and said,
Behold my mother and my brethren! For whosoever
shall do the will of my Father which is in heaven, the
same is my brother, and sister, and mother (Mathew
12:46-50).

There came then his brethren and his mother, and,
standing without, sent unto him, calling him. And the
multitude sat about him, and they said unto him, Behold,
thy mother and thy brethren without seek for thee.

And he answered them, saying, Who is my mother,
or my brethren? And he looked round about on them
which sat about him, and said, Behold my mother and
my brethren! For whosoever shall do the will of God,
the same is my brother, and my sister, and mother
(Mark 3:31-35).

Is not this the carpenter, the son of Mary, the brother
of James, and Joses, and of Juda, and Simon? and are
not his sisters here with us? And they were offended
at him (Mark 6:3).

You can clearly see that Jesus biological family was recognized here
but Jesus demonstrates that His true family, are those who do the
will of His heavenly Father.

Another scripture shows Jesus handing the reigns of head of
household over to His oldest brother. It is assumed that Joseph has

passed away by this time and Jesus has been the head of household and responsible for the wellbeing of His mother.

> When Jesus therefore saw his mother, and the disciple standing by, whom he loved, he saith unto his mother, Woman, behold thy son! Then saith he to the disciple, Behold thy mother! And from that hour that disciple took her unto his own *home.* (John 19:26-27)

Then the Apostle Paul identifies James as the brother of the Lord in his Letter to the Galatians.

> But other of the apostles saw I none, save James the Lord's brother. (Galatians 1:19)

Other scriptures link other men to be Jesus' brothers but they are not as clear and since names are common, they may not be accurate. It is accepted that large families in those days were common.

~~~

# Chapter 6

# Church

*"A good church is a Bible-centered church. Nothing is as important as this--not a large congregation, a witty pastor, or tangible experiences of the Holy Spirit." Alistair Begg*

1. What and where is the true Church of GOD established by GOD in the bible?
2. Why are there more religious missionaries in religious parts of the United States than atheist or agnostic communities?
3. Why should I tithe 10% of my income to church?

**Q.** What and where is the true Church of GOD established by
GOD in the bible?

**A.** This is an excellent question. The answer is that the one true
Church has no physical location because it is not a building nor
is it a single denomination because not one denomination has
been able to reach the entire world's population.

The lord has His people sealed and they consist of every believer
who has called upon the name of the Lord. They, myself included,
make up the body of Christ and we are not all in one accord, yet.

The Bible says that, "whosoever calls upon the Lord shall be saved"
(Acts 2:21). But, "Till we all come in the unity of the faith, and of the
knowledge of the Son of God, unto a perfect man, unto the measure
of the stature of the fullness of Christ:" (Ephesians 4:13). "We can be
confident of this very thing, that he which hath begun a good work
in you will perform it until the day of Jesus Christ" (Philippians1:6).

Remember it is the Lords church and He is building it. The following
verses show that it is the Father who reveals Jesus Christ to us.

> 13 When Jesus came into the coasts of Caesarea
> Philippi, he asked his disciples, saying, Whom do
> men say that I the Son of man am?
>
> 14 And they said, Some say that thou art John the
> Baptist: some, Elias; and others, Jeremias, or one of
> the prophets.
>
> 15 He saith unto them, But whom say ye that I am?
>
> 16 And Simon Peter answered and said, Thou art the
> Christ, the Son of the living God.

17 And Jesus answered and said unto him, Blessed art thou, Simon Barjona: for flesh and blood hath not revealed it unto thee, but my Father which is in heaven. 18 And I say also unto thee, That thou art Peter, and upon this rock I will build my church; and the gates of hell shall not prevail against it. 19 And I will give unto thee the keys of the kingdom of heaven: and whatsoever thou shalt bind on earth shall be bound in heaven: and whatsoever thou shalt loose on earth shall be loosed in heaven.

20 Then charged he his disciples that they should tell no man that he was Jesus the Christ.

21 From that time forth began Jesus to shew unto his disciples- (Mathew 16:13-21a)

Notice in verse 18 when He says "upon this rock" the rock He speaks of is not Peter but the words He spoke to Peter saying "Blessed art thou - for flesh and blood hath not reveled this to you, but MY FATHER." You see, it is the revelation knowledge that Jesus is the Lord, the Son of the Living God, the Anointed, the Christ, and the only wise God. On this knowledge is HIS CHURCH built, which He purchased with HIS OWN BLOOD. This is the one true church, on Earth, that the Bible speaks of.

*I left off part of vs. 21 because when you become a part of the Rock then from that time forth Jesus will begin to show you all you need to know.*

~~~

**Q.** Why are there more religious missionaries in religious parts of the United States than atheist or agnostic communities?

This is based on experience and therefore contains assumptions but I think it's a fair assessment that religious missionaries are far more prevalent, present, and visible in area of the United States like the "bible belt" vs. parts of the country considered less religious. I'm missing why that might be the case; missionaries are supposed to bring religion (no?) and converting other popular religions must be more challenging.

**A.** Unless the missionary has some Church behind him/her for financial support, it is simply a matter of location. Christians who are faithful and read their Bibles will often feel a desire for missions work but are unable to relocate do to circumstance. They also look around their hometowns and realize that there is a mission field right there. Some of us even get on the internet and spread the Gospel. This is the seed principle of evangelism, by sharing we never know how the Lord will use what we put out, or whose lives we may touch.

I personally feel led to go to Haiti and work the mission fields there. For now, I am working through the internet and when/where ever opportunities open up I share my faith. Sometimes I think I make a difference, other times I feel as if I wasted my breath. In any case I am only responsible to tell the truth, not for where it lands. or how it is received. Sometimes I think I am following Jonah's path and God has me in a big fish waiting to spew me out on the shore because I am afraid to go there on my own.

~~~

**Q.** Why should I tithe 10% of my income to church?

What does it do? It's like a hard concept for me to grasp. But then again, I haven't really *read* the bible; just hear a quote here and there.

**A.** Unless you are a believer then tithing probably will not do anything for you, especially if you are not happy to give it. If however you are a believer then I suggest reading Malachi. It is the last book of the Old Testament; before the New Testament. The portion that deals specifically with tithing is listed below.

> Will a man rob God? Yet ye have robbed me. But ye say, Wherein have we robbed thee? In tithes and offerings. Ye are cursed with a curse: for ye have robbed me, even this whole nation.

> Bring ye all the tithes into the storehouse, that there may be meat in mine house, and prove me now herewith, saith the LORD of hosts, if I will not open you the windows of heaven, and pour you out a blessing, that there shall not be room enough to receive it. And I will rebuke the devourer for your sakes, and he shall not destroy the fruits of your ground; neither shall your vine cast her fruit before the time in the field, saith the LORD of hosts. And all nations shall call you blessed: for ye shall be a delightsome land, saith the LORD of hosts (Malachi 3:8-12).

Essentially this was written for the Jews under the old covenant but it is still relevant because God says he does not change in both the Old and New Testaments, read Malachi 3:6, and Hebrews 13:8. The curse spoken of means that because you are not in obedience to God in tithing then the world will work against you. It is not a "God is gonna get you for not tithing" as much as it is about having the blessings of God in your life because you are tithing. Especially those mentioned in the passages I posted here. Those blessings are meant to spill over and touch everyone you come into contact with.

Tithing is the only place in the scripture where the Lord challenges the believer to "Prove Him." Proving God to yourself in this manner is a blessing that is quite unique because God opens "you" as a window of heaven and poor "you" out to other people in such abundance that there will not be enough room to receive it. If you can receive what I am saying here, then look at the passage again. God is saying that He will rebuke things that come to devour your fruit, and He will ensure that your fruit is on time. The fruit mentioned in the passage can be taken as the spiritual fruit spoken of in Galatians 5:22-23 and Ephesians 5:9 but it also includes the fruit of your labors, this means financial blessings. Of course these promises are made for obedience to tithes and offerings, not just tithes.

That is what your tithe does for you and through you personally. But what it also does is pay the bills of the church. Supports missionaries through the Church and if you have a full time Pastor then it will also pay his salary and any staff that works there. Some of the funds may go back into the community as well. Many churches offer scholar ships to local colleges for some of their members. Some sponsor soup kitchens or care packages for emergencies and disaster relief. You should be able to ask your pastor how the money is being used. As a member you should also have an annual meeting where the pastor and board members give an account of the funds. This should include how much was collected and how it was spent. Some churches may even allow the congregation to vote on the budget.

At no time should you ever be made to feel obligated to tithe. God intended tithing to be a blessing both for you and through you. Any action you are guilted into for a church or other cause did not come from God and so there will be no blessing in it. This is why Jesus overturned the table in the temple. If you are operating outside of faith then you are better off holding on to your money and finding a church that will teach you how to operate in faith.

~~~

# Chapter 7

# Theology

*"I know that some are always studying the meaning of the fourth toe of the right foot of some beast in prophecy and have never used either foot to go and bring men to Christ. I do not know who the 666 is in Revelation but I know the world is sick, sick, sick and the best way to speed the Lord's return is to win more souls for Him." Vance Havner*

1. Is there hard scientific evidence that can support the theory of a personal God?
2. If the Bible is inerrant then why does God allow errors in the Interpretation?
3. Have we been arrogant by thinking we should "accept Christ" as compared to running after the King?
4. Why did Abraham sacrifice his son?
5. Why do Christians trust in the word of a former murderer, Paul (Saul of Tarsus)?
6. Do believers truly believe that nonbelievers will suffer an unimaginable fate after death?
7. The bible says 1/3 of mankind will be killed in the near future. How is this likely going to happen?
8. Does it matter if free will exists?
9. What does it mean to, not cast your pearls before the swine?
10. If God is benevolent, then who is He to send someone to hell?
11. What precisely was the knowledge that God didn't want Adam and Eve to have?
12. How did the Israelites wandering in the desert for 40 years work logistically?

13. Why didn't God deal with Adam and Eve's sin in the beginning and save us all this suffering?

14. Did Adam and Eve have children who practiced incest to create children to populate the earth?

15. Were Adam and Eve genetically identical?

16. What do religious texts specify as the reason for Bathsheba to give into King David's seduction?

17. Will the Rapture help restore ecological balance to the Earth?

18. What does God have to say about technology?

19. How can you prove that Jesus really died on the cross and came back to life three days later?

**Q.** Is there hard scientific evidence that can support the theory of a personal God?

Is there an intelligent position out there that can support the theory of a personal god that uses the most advanced method of discerning truth we've devised, the scientific method, by presenting hard evidence for that theory?

A leap of faith does not cut it. Faith must be supported by evidence, otherwise it is just blind.

**A.** I am sure if you keep looking, you will find some evidence that your personal god is real, I will bet he is very predictable too. I mean after all science is predictable you do the same thing and get the same result. Unfortunately for you, the god you will find is not the God you are looking for.

The God you are looking for is sovereign and cannot be found without faith. The Bible makes this clear in the following verses.

> Now the just shall live by faith: but if any man draw back, my soul shall have no pleasure in him. (Hebrews 10:38)

> Now faith is the substance of things hoped for, the evidence of things not seen. (Hebrews 11:1)

> But without faith it is impossible to please him: for he that cometh to God must believe that he is, and that he is a rewarder of them that diligently seek him. (Hebrews 11:6)

> But that no man is justified by the law in the sight of God, it is evident: for, The just shall live by faith. (Galatians 3:11)

For therein is the righteousness of God revealed from faith to faith: as it is written, The just shall live by faith. (Romans 1:17)

If any of you lack wisdom, let him ask of God, that giveth to all men liberally, and upbraideth not; and it shall be given him. But let him ask in faith, nothing wavering. For he that wavereth is like a wave of the sea driven with the wind and tossed. For let not that man think that he shall receive any thing of the Lord. (James 1:5-7)

Just remember if you persist in a search for God outside of faith there are plenty of gods willing to pop up and say "hey look here it's me; god." Is that the god you choose?

~~~

**Q.** If the Bible is inerrant then why does God allow errors in the Interpretation?

Why do some Christians believe that God would not allow errors in the Bible but would somehow allow errors in its interpretation?

There is an idea that some Christians believe that the scripture is inerrant because God himself guided the editors. However, when asked about the inquisition and other aspect of Christianity that are no longer politically correct, some Christians believe that it is an error in interpretation by His followers.

So why would God allow some kinds of errors and not others? Why would a God that doesn't allow error in scriptures allow error in interpreting of the scriptures?

Most popular versions of scriptures change all the time. Sometimes some verses show up in King James Version only to be found later that it's not in the oldest manuscript. Does God intend that certain uncertainty would determine if a verse should be part of Holy Scripture or not?

**A.** The simple answer is in the pages of scriptures themselves. We are told here, that the scriptures are inspired by God and can be trusted for the purpose of learning and instructions. The Apostle Paul writes;

> All scripture is given by inspiration of God, and is profitable for doctrine, for reproof, for correction, for instruction in righteousness: That the man of God may be perfect, thoroughly furnished unto all good works (2Timothy 3:16-17).

So why is it possible that they can be misinterpreted? It is because vain and self-serving men choose to ignore Gods warnings and ignore His advice. The Lord tells us,

> Trust in the LORD with all thine heart; and lean not unto thine own understanding. In all thy ways acknowledge him, and he shall direct thy paths. Be not wise in thine own eyes: fear the LORD, and depart from evil (Proverbs 3:5-7).

He does not give us full knowledge all at once either. Some things are just beyond human understanding. Hear what He says through His prophet Isaiah:

> Whom shall he teach knowledge? and whom shall he make to understand doctrine? them that are weaned from the milk, and drawn from the breasts. For precept must be upon precept, precept upon precept;

line upon line, line upon line; here a little, and there
a little: For with stammering lips and another tongue
will he speak to this people (Isaiah 28:9-11).

Ultimately, God desires to have a relationship with us individually
although He also deals with us collectively. He says; "Draw nigh to
God, and he will draw nigh to you. Cleanse your hands, ye sinners;
and purify your hearts, ye double minded" (James 4:8).

People who seem to say the right words, do not fool God. He knows
the hearts of those who love Him and the hearts of those that teach
false doctrines, or as you asked, misinterpret the Bible.

Wherefore the Lord said, Forasmuch as this people
draw near me with their mouth, and with their lips
do honour me, but have removed their heart far from
me, and their fear toward me is taught by the precept
of men (Isaiah 29:13).

Those who humble themselves and seek the Lord in faith with a
repentant heart will be brought to a full understanding of who He is.

~~~

**Q.** Have we been arrogant by thinking we should "accept Christ"
as compared to running after the King?

We seriously need to stop acting like we should "accept Christ"
and realize we should follow Christ. Let's get over ourselves

**A.** I do not see how accepting something that is contrary to
natural thinking could be considered arrogant. The way I
understand it is that accepting Christ is an act of repentance or
an acknowledgement of His Lordship.

As for following Christ, can anyone truly do that? I have a relationship with the Lord and I still fail miserably. Yet; He promised to never leave us or forsake us. I am responsible for what I clearly understand, but much is still like looking through that dark glass. I have also seen that much of what I thought I knew; God had to show me how wrong I was.

I have at times given my last dollar but I also knew I had a payday. I have never plucked out my eyes, or cut off my hand or foot. I still don't understand all of His parables or everything in the book of revelation. The best I can do is live by the faith I have and allow Christ to work in me. I trust the Lord; if that is something besides acceptance then maybe I misunderstand your question.

I think maybe it is arrogant to think we can just follow after Christ in the power of our mind or flesh. Jesus was kept on the path by angels. "For he shall give his angels charge over thee, to keep thee in all thy ways" (Psalm 91:11).

~~~

**Q.** Why did Abraham sacrifice his son?

In Abraham's mind how could he justify following through with it?

On the one hand, there is his faith and confidence in the word of God and on the other taking the life of an innocent child who did him no harm? How could a good God take the life of an innocent child? How does he justify the two sides of the equation? What of Isaac; is he merely a pawn in this dialogue or is there something more to this?

**A.** Abraham's experience with God went deeper than what you see just casually reading the Genesis account of his life. He likely thought that Isaac was the Messiah. Just how much of what God shared with him or how much he knew about the coming Messiah is unknown. However, it is clear Abraham believed that God could raise Isaac from the dead.

The New Testament writer gives us this revelation,

> By faith Abraham, when he was tried, offered up Isaac: and he that had received the promises offered up his only begotten son, of whom it was said, That in Isaac shall thy seed be called: Accounting that God was able to raise him up, even from the dead; from whence also he received him in a figure (Hebrews 11:17-19).

Now let me Paraphrase it and replace a few pronouns with proper nouns.

> When Abraham was tried, Isaac was offered up because Abraham had received a promise by faith that in Isaac _Abraham's messiah_ shall be called. So Abraham offered up his only begotten son Isaac, accounting that God was able to raise Isaac up, even from the dead; from whence also Abraham received the Messiah in a figure (Hebrews 11:17-19 paraphrased).

Abraham's courageous actions were enough for God to go forth with His plan through Isaac. The world owes Abraham and Isaac a great debt. God bless them even now.

> The LORD had said unto Abram, Get thee out of thy country, and from thy kindred, and from thy father's house, unto a land that I will shew thee. And I will make of thee a great nation, and I will bless thee, and make thy name great; and thou shalt be a blessing: And I will bless them that bless thee, and curse him

that curseth thee: and in thee shall all families of the earth be blessed (Genesis 12:1-3).

And God said unto Abraham, Let it not be grievous in thy sight because of the lad, and because of thy bondwoman; in all that Sarah hath said unto thee, hearken unto her voice; for in Isaac shall thy seed be called. (Genesis 21:12)

~~~

**Q.** Why do Christians trust in the word of a former murderer, Paul (Saul of Tarsus)?

So much of modern Christian belief is based on the letters of Paul, who was formerly, by his own words, responsible for the deaths of many early Christians. He might not have executed them personally, but he gave the authority to have them killed.

"And I persecuted this way unto the death, binding and delivering into prisons both men and women" (Acts 22:4).

When it comes down to it, were his actions much different from Osama bin Laden's? Both were led by misguided religious ideology to kill hundreds of innocent people of an opposing faith. Neither man directly killed others, but by their authority, had them killed.

If bin Laden had converted to Christianity later in life, would any Christian be forgiving enough to accept him as a prominent Christian leader?

**A.** Paul or formerly Saul of Tarsus, spent several years as a Christian before he walked in the role of the Apostle. Jesus says "except you become as a little child." This is true for everyone and Saul was no different. Neither would Osama be if he had accepted Jesus as his lord.

Paul himself taught that to be involved even in the lowest offices of Christian leadership you must have these qualifications.

> 1 This *is* a true saying, If a man desire the office of a bishop, he desireth a good work. 2 A bishop then must be blameless, the husband of one wife, vigilant, sober, of good behaviour, given to hospitality, apt to teach; 3Not given to wine, no striker, not greedy of filthy lucre; but patient, not a brawler, not covetous; 4 One that ruleth well his own house, having his children in subjection with all gravity; 5 (For if a man know not how to rule his own house, how shall he take care of the church of God?)

> 6 Not a novice, lest being lifted up with pride he fall into the condemnation of the devil. 7 Moreover he must have a good report of them which are without; lest he fall into reproach and the snare of the devil.

> 8 Likewise *must* the deacons *be* grave, not doubletongued, not given to much wine, not greedy of filthy lucre; 9 Holding the mystery of the faith in a pure conscience. 10 And let these also first be proved; then let them use the office of a deacon, being *found* blameless (1Timothy 3:1-10).

Notice verse 6 says, "not a novice" which is my first point, a novice is basically untested, and until they have actually worked through a few trials as a Christian, they lack the experience to lead people who are going through trials.

Probably one of the toughest things for those desiring to enter into ministry is to have a good reputation among nonbelievers; *(see vs. 7)*. This doesn't mean you have to get them to like you or agree with you, but that they can find no legitimate fault in your conduct. To answer your question...

> If bin Laden had converted to Christianity later in life, would any Christian be forgiving enough to accept him as a prominent Christian leader? *(Sic)*

Yes if he truly converted and God called him to leadership.

~~~

**Q.** Do believers truly believe that nonbelievers will suffer an unimaginable fate after death?

Go to a Hell-like place. Exist in Limbo, etc. If so, why do they believe that?

**A.** Christians that believe the Bible believe that non-believers will suffer in a place commonly referred to as hell. We believe that Jesus is the Son of God, sent to warn all men of the consequences of following the gods of this world and especially if you are a god unto yourself. Jesus spoke of hell authoritatively, which was unprecedented, as no other religion that taught about hell could give as clear and definite description. He described Hell as a place of torments without relief and without reprieve until the Day of Judgment.

He tells us, "It is not God's will that any should perish but that all should come to the knowledge of God and His salvation" (2Peter 3:9 *paraphrased*). He made it simple to be saved, saying that if anyone will believe in Him they would not perish but have everlasting life. He then volunteered to give His sinless life as a ransom for all the sins of those who put their faith in Him. You do not have to work or make promises. God's love for you will take care of all the changes you will go through and yes, you will start changing but it is not a difficult or punitive unless you make it difficult. The reality is God wants you to lead a good and productive life that you will enjoy and one He can be proud of. Jesus is looking forward to meeting you.

Scripture References about hell. (This is not a complete list).

> And if thy hand offend thee, cut it off: it is better for thee to enter into life maimed, than having two hands to go into hell, into the fire that never shall be quenched: Where their worm dieth not, and the fire is not quenched. And if thy foot offend thee, cut it off: it is better for thee to enter halt into life, than having two feet to be cast into hell, into the fire that never shall be quenched: Where their worm dieth not, and the fire is not quenched. And if thine eye offend thee, pluck it out: it is better for thee to enter into the kingdom of God with one eye, than having two eyes to be cast into hell fire: Where their worm dieth not, and the fire is not quenched. For every one shall be salted with fire, and every sacrifice shall be salted with salt (Mark 9:43-49).

> But I will forewarn you whom ye shall fear: Fear him, which after he hath killed hath power to cast into hell; yea, I say unto you, Fear him (Luke 12:5).

Now this next passage is a story Jesus told.

> There was a certain rich man, which was clothed in purple and fine linen, and fared sumptuously every day: And there was a certain beggar named Lazarus, which was laid at his gate, full of sores, And desiring to

be fed with the crumbs which fell from the rich man's table: moreover the dogs came and licked his sores.

And it came to pass, that the beggar died, and was carried by the angels into Abraham's bosom: the rich man also died, and was buried; And in hell he lift up his eyes, being in torments, and seeth Abraham afar off, and Lazarus in his bosom. And he cried and said, Father Abraham, have mercy on me, and send Lazarus, that he may dip the tip of his finger in water, and cool my tongue; for I am tormented in this flame.

But Abraham said, Son, remember that thou in thy lifetime receivedst thy good things, and likewise Lazarus evil things: but now he is comforted, and thou art tormented. And beside all this, between us and you there is a great gulf fixed: so that they which would pass from hence to you cannot; neither can they pass to us, that *would come* from thence.

Then he said, I pray thee therefore, father, that thou wouldest send him to my father's house: For I have five brethren; that he may testify unto them, lest they also come into this place of torment.

Abraham saith unto him, They have Moses and the prophets; let them hear them.

And he said, Nay, father Abraham: but if one went unto them from the dead, they will repent.

And he said unto him, If they hear not Moses and the prophets, neither will they be persuaded, though one rose from the dead (Luke 16:19-31).

Gods Plan of Salvation,

> And as Moses lifted up the serpent in the wilderness, even so must the Son of man be lifted up: That whosoever believeth in him should not perish, but have eternal life. For God so loved the world, that he gave his only begotten Son, that whosoever believeth in him should not perish, but have everlasting life. For God sent not his Son into the world to condemn the world; but that the world through him might be saved. He that believeth on him is not condemned: but he that believeth not is condemned already, because he hath not believed in the name of the only begotten Son of God.

> And this is the condemnation, that light is come into the world, and men loved darkness rather than light, because their deeds were evil. For every one that doeth evil hateth the light, neither cometh to the light, lest his deeds should be reproved. But he that doeth truth cometh to the light, that his deeds may be made manifest, that they are wrought in God (John 3:14-21).

> For they being ignorant of God's righteousness, and going about to establish their own righteousness, have not submitted themselves unto the righteousness of God. For Christ *is* the end of the law for righteousness to every one that believeth. For Moses describeth the righteousness which is of the law, That the man which doeth those things shall live by them.

> But the righteousness which is of faith speaketh on this wise, Say not in thine heart, Who shall ascend into heaven? (that is, to bring Christ down *from above:*) Or, Who shall descend into the deep? (that is, to bring up Christ again from the dead.)

But what saith it? The word is nigh thee, *even* in thy mouth, and in thy heart: that is, the word of faith, which we preach; That if thou shalt confess with thy mouth the Lord Jesus, and shalt believe in thine heart that God hath raised him from the dead, thou shalt be saved. For with the heart man believeth unto righteousness; and with the mouth confession is made unto salvation. For the scripture saith, Whosoever believeth on him shall not be ashamed (Romans 10:3-11).

~~~

**Q.** The bible says 1/3 of mankind will be killed in the near future. How is this likely going to happen?

A third of mankind was killed by the three plagues of fire, smoke and sulfur that came out of their mouths (Revelation 9:18). How is this likely going to happen? Will this be the result of a war, or something unimaginable caused by God? And does this literal mean 1/3 of the current population?

**A.** Well first, let us read the scriptures before and after Revelations 9:18 that directly address your question.

12 One woe is past; *and,* behold, there come two woes more hereafter. 13 And the sixth angel sounded, and I heard a voice from the four horns of the golden altar which is before God, And the four angels were loosed, which were prepared for an hour, and a day, and a month, and a year, for to slay the third part of men. 16 And the number of the army of the horsemen *were* two hundred thousand thousand: and I heard the number of them. 17 And thus I saw the horses in the vision, and them that sat on them, having breastplates

of fire, and of jacinth, and brimstone: and the heads of the horses *were* as the heads of lions; and out of their mouths issued fire and smoke and brimstone. 18 By these three was the third part of men killed, by the fire, and by the smoke, and by the brimstone, which issued out of their mouths. 19 For their power is in their mouth, and in their tails: for their tails *were* like unto serpents, and had heads, and with them they do hurt. 20 And the rest of the men which were not killed by these plagues yet repented not of the works of their hands, that they should not worship devils, and idols of gold, and silver, and brass, and stone, and of wood: which neither can see, nor hear, nor walk: 21Neither repented they of their murders, nor of their sorceries, nor of their fornication, nor of their thefts (Revelations 9:12-21).

Very often scripture is symbolic, since this was a vision, then we may also be dealing with John's interpretation of what he saw. Some of the beasts John described could be our modern machines, or even some futuristic machine. In this particular case though, these beasts are "horses," probably some sort of heavily armored land vehicles, with a cannon capable of launching explosives and rear mounted weapons that are either manned or have some type of computers capable of targeting and firing upon any army trying to attack from the rear. The description of the armor of the operators almost sounds like some sort of force field, "Fire and jacinth," there will be 200 million of these machines and as of yet I do not know of any Middle Eastern country that has the facilities to produce that kind of machinery. However, when they collaborate I suppose they could. The four angels that are loosed represent four nations along the Euphrates River that have been holding hostilities towards the rest of the world. The most likely candidates are Saudi Arabia, Iraq, Turkey, and Syria, all of which are Muslim majority nations.

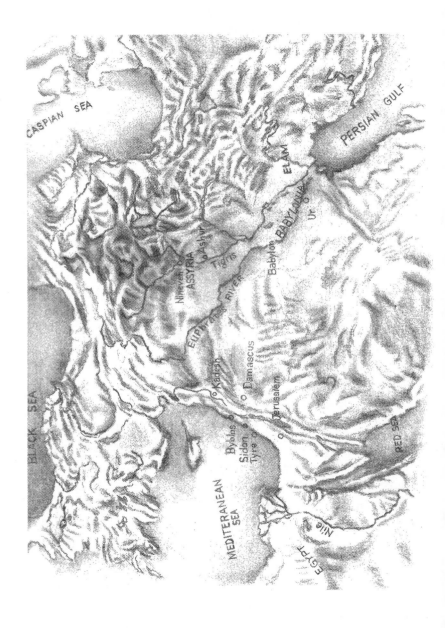

It is important to realize that at this point all the Christians will have been removed "raptured." Still there will be people who will receive the Lord, namely the "very elect" which Jesus said would survive this ordeal. The Bible says they are 144,000 Jews. 12,000 from each of the tribes of Israel and they are all virgin men. I believe these will also lead millions more to the Lord. Many of whom will be martyred. It is because the Christians are gone that so much evil is capable of coming to power.

I personally believe that before any of this happens there will be one last worldwide revival. This one will have a huge impact and billions of people will receive Jesus as their Lord. This is the purpose of each of the visits in Jesus parable of the wages.

> 1 For the kingdom of heaven is like unto a man *that is* an householder, which went out early in the morning to hire labourers into his vineyard. 2 And when he had agreed with the labourers for a penny a day, he sent them into his vineyard. And he went out about the third hour, and saw others standing idle in the marketplace, 4 And said unto them; Go ye also into the vineyard, and whatsoever is right I will give you. And they went their way. 5 Again he went out about the sixth and ninth hour, and did likewise. 6 And about the eleventh hour he went out, and found others standing idle, and saith unto them, Why stand ye here all the day idle? 7 They say unto him, Because no man hath hired us. He saith unto them, Go ye also into the vineyard; and whatsoever is right, *that* shall ye receive (Mathew 20:1-7).

When this revival has reached every soul with the Gospel, then the rapture will take place. Those that believed will be caught up and avoid this great tribulation.

~~~

**Q.** Does it matter if free will exists?

If so in what ways?

I've seen a lot of chatter around questions of free will—was wondering as to the relevancy of the debate in regard to practical matters of the everyday? If it exists (or not), how does that affect one's actions in either case? From a philosophical or quotidian perspective, I'm not sure I see the relevance so please feel free to share any insights.

**A.** I think the more complex the thinker the freer they are and the more it matters. There is such a plethora of diverse minds and thinkers and many of them would give you a unique answer to this very question. Of course, no one is completely free. We all have some constraints some are inner workings of a moral consciousness, some are behaviors taught by an environment. But, it is evident to me that people can break either of these or any constraints. A person who has been victimized by abuses can by their own choices overcome the conditioning or fall prey to it. There appears to be no solid scientific evidence that can predict how a person will respond to whatever stimulus is available.

Let us look at a far simpler life form, the ant; ant's behaviors are pretty predictable. If you place a sugar cube in the path of an ant the ant will follow the path from the sugar cube back along the precise trail to their hive and tell all the other ants how to get to the sugar cube. All the ants will then follow that path but if you put obstacles along the path, each ant will try a different path to overcome the obstacle and get back to the trail. This demonstrates a limited amount of free will combined with a pretty tight script that it will follow to complete a task. When any particular ant gets back on the trail, it will continue to use the new path even if you remove the obstacle. So, does it matter to the ants, probably not.

Humans behave similarly when they are confronted with obstacles. Our free will comes into play on how we will overcome the obstacle will we follow a moral script, a learned and expected script or will we get creative and discover something unprecedented. Humans are amazing in this capacity to go their own way. But, on occasion I think we get a little mysterious help from our maker especially if we believe in Him and are not bound up in religious rituals.

Why does it matter? In an individual free will can help them to grow and make better decisions for themselves. If they are bound to a script this keeps things pretty much the same we would not have developed things like electricity. We would have fled from fire rather than learned to control it. On a civil level, free will gives us the right to set standards of acceptable behavior and the right to enforce those standards against the will of transgressors.

In Christianity, to think that free will does not exist is to make God to be a tyrant who created life only to torment it. There could not be any real purpose in that because life issues from God and He would not desire to torment himself. He created Life and placed some boundaries in it to preserve it. Free will then makes us responsible for ignoring those boundaries and thus responsible for our own lives. Seeing that we all have fallen God provided a path back and sent messengers to us to guide us back to life. It is our free choice to make. The Bible says, "I call heaven and earth to record this day against you, *that* I have set before you life and death, blessing and cursing: therefore choose life, that both thou and thy seed may live:"(Deuteronomy 30:19).

~~~

**Q.** What does it mean to, not cast your pearls before the swine?

I am referencing Mathew 7:6 "Give not that which is holy unto the dogs, neither cast ye your pearls before swine, lest they trample them under their feet, and turn again and rend you."

**A.** Jesus is using symbolism so that His words could easily be carried through the ages. To get the deepest intent of what Jesus meant we need to identify what is "holy," what is "the dogs," what is "your pearls," and what is "swine"?

"That which is holy," is the revelation knowledge of God's word. Especially if it concerns whom Jesus is; but can be broadened to include the things the Lord has shown you in your personal walk of faith.

The "dogs" are those who once followed Jesus but then turned back to their old ways.

> For it had been better for them not to have known the way of righteousness, than, after they have known *it,* to turn from the holy commandment delivered unto them. But it is happened unto them according to the true proverb, The dog *is* turned to his own vomit again; and the sow that was washed to her wallowing in the mire. (2Peter 2:21-22)

Another thing about dogs is they beg. I gave a lesson about this in another question, when a woman came begging to Jesus and He called her a dog. Your faith is "Holy Bread" not to be cast to beggars. I will talk about that sow a little later.

The "pearls" are representative of being adorned with godliness, wisdom, and good works. Pearls are formed when something uncomfortable enters into an oyster. Over time the oyster layers it with a silky substance and it grows and grows each new layer adding value to the pearl. God's word is like that. When we first receive it, it makes us uncomfortable. Overtime it grows, and grows layer by layer. It will never truly feel comfortable to us, but it will make us more and more valuable to Jesus. Another way to look at is that when we receive Jesus, we are like that piece of grit in the oyster. We make the worldly people feel discomfort, but God continues to add layers of wisdom to us. As we grow in it, we become of great value to both the world, and to God.

Jesus compared the kingdom of heaven to a man who went and sold all he had to purchase a single pearl of great price.

> Again, the kingdom of heaven is like unto a merchant man, seeking goodly pearls: Who, when he had found one pearl of great price, went and sold all that he had, and bought it (Mathew 13:45).

The pearl Jesus referred to is a lost soul that Jesus purchased on the cross.

However, in most references to pearls throughout the scriptures it is teaching us that they are not as valuable as God's wisdom. The book of revelation describes a great evil city that is adorned as a woman in pearls (Revelation 18:16). In this instance, pearls would represent earthly or worldly wisdom.

One of my favorite things to see a woman wear are pearls. To me they are more attractive than precious stones. Never-the-less, scripture teaches that although these things are valuable they are not to be worn as a showpiece in churches.

> In like manner also, that women adorn themselves in modest apparel, with shamefacedness and sobriety;

not with broided hair, or gold, or pearls, or costly array; 10 But (which becometh women professing godliness) with good works (1Timothy 2:9).

This shows that doing good works is like wearing pearls. Your deeds in Christ will shine on their own. You do not have to boast on them.

The "swine" is the last symbol on the list. Swine or pigs were forbidden as meat to the Jews. All of the dietary laws had symbolic meanings. The swine are unclean because they have cloven hooves, and do not chew the cud. This juxtaposes religious teachers who look holy in the eyes of men, but do not meditate on God's word. They can be summed up in the saying "they walk the walk, but they do not talk the talk." We also know that pigs will eat the roots of plants, thus killing the plant because it has destroyed its ability to draw nutrients. They are like religious busybodies that will dig into your life and root up your past to make themselves appear good.

So to answer your question about Mathew 7:6 "Give not that which is holy unto the dogs, neither cast ye your pearls before swine, lest they trample them under their feet, and turn again and rend you."

Let me paraphrase it like this;

"Do not share your daily walk with God with backsliders who are living their old life. Neither expose the things God has taught you, nor your good works with people who like to look as if they know more than you do. They could use it to undermine your calling, and labors of love in Christ, bringing up your flaws and discourage others from following your good example, leaving you feeling unworthy and broken."

~~~

**Q.** If God is benevolent, then who is He to send someone to hell?

Is sending someone to eternal torture benevolent?

**A.** God's benevolence is evident in that He made a way to escape hell for anyone who will accept it. He makes no demands on the sinner, except to accept His gift of grace, by believing in His son Jesus. If it is not enough that God has given you life then consider that He decided to pay off your sin debt. You are probably thinking, well I have not really done anything so bad to have to spend an eternity in Hell. But, I want you to think about a few things...

According to the Bible, God, who is HOLY and an All Powerful Entity, became human. He suffered and died as a human, but He lived a perfect sinless life. Why would He do that?

It was not something Jesus wanted to do so He prayed to His Father:

> Then cometh Jesus with them unto a place called Gethsemane, and saith unto the disciples, Sit ye here, while I go and pray yonder. And he took with him Peter and the two sons of Zebedee, and began to be sorrowful and very heavy. Then saith he unto them, My soul is exceeding sorrowful, even unto death: tarry ye here, and watch with me. And he went a little further, and fell on his face, and prayed, saying, O my Father, if it be possible, let this cup pass from me: nevertheless not as I will, but as thou wilt (Mathew 26:36-39).

His decision was not based on His will but on His benevolence. He volunteered to be tortured and killed so He could stand before all mighty God and say Father I forgive them. This sacrifice was made for everyone but it is up to you to accept it. If you refuse, He has no choice but to refuse you on the Day of Judgment. He will not allow you to continue living forever with your sin in Heaven with Him. Whether or not anyone will suffer for eternity I cannot say for sure. The one thing I can tell you is that everyone who refuses to accept His salvation will be cast into the Lake of fire, along with everything that is evil. That is called the second death.

You may say why can't He put us some place where we can go on living? The answer is that you would have to spend eternity carrying your sin completely separated from God. The sin that is in you would not be cured. It would cause you to become depressed or mean and it would grow worse and worse. Imagine living for all eternity all alone, susceptible to pain and diseases, just wishing you could die but never being able to.

~~~

**Q.** What precisely was the knowledge that God didn't want Adam and Eve to have?

It must have been very threatening to God considering His reaction to the eating of the "forbidden fruit." Over the years, I have seen many contradictory attempts at explaining what precisely this knowledge was. The only one that ever made any intellectual sense to me can be found in Daniel Quinn's novel Ishmael.

**A.** First lets read the text in question:

26 And God said, Let us make man in our image, after our likeness: and let them have dominion over the fish of the sea, and over the fowl of the air, and over the cattle, and over all the earth, and over every creeping thing that creepeth upon the earth.

27 So God created man in his own image, in the image of God created he him; male and female created he them.

28 And God blessed them, and God said unto them, Be fruitful, and multiply, and replenish the earth, and subdue it: and have dominion over the fish of the sea, and over the fowl of the air, and over every living thing that moveth upon the earth. (Genesis 1:26-28)

Let me be clear here, it had nothing to do with sex. God had already told them to be fruitful and multiply. In verse 26 and in verse 28 we see that even before He made man He planned that there would be many of us. Sex was not the original sin nor did God call the act itself evil. He does call lust evil and lust comes in many forms. Sex is one of them but when we speak of lust it covers a plethora of appetites that a person can become addicted to.

So if it is not sex, then is it lusts? No! It was precisely what God said it was, "the knowledge to distinguish between right and wrong." You see evil was already in existence, but the existence itself could not tempt man to participate in evil. As long as humanity obeyed God, they would never have sinned. We have always had free will to do anything we wanted to; it never would have entered conscious thought to do anything that God forbade.

Once Adam and Eve heard the lie and believed it God knew that they would never stop being disobedient. He was right, but it was not because God felt threatened that He sent them out of the garden. It was because He loved us. You see if humans could live forever while they are tainted with sin, it is only a matter of time before we begin to feel the effects of it in our bodies. Diseases and injuries would cause us an eternity of sorrow. That is why God did not want us to partake of the "Tree of Life" until He could cleanse us of sin.

> And the LORD God said, Behold, the man is become as one of us, to know good and evil. and now, lest he put forth his hand, and take also of the tree of life, and eat, and live for ever: Therefore the LORD God sent him forth from the garden of Eden, to till the ground from whence he was taken. So he drove out the man; and he placed at the east of the garden of Eden Cherubims, and a flaming sword which turned every way, to keep the way of the tree of life (Genesis 3:22-24).

As for the effects of sin, well I think that is self-evident.

~~~

**Q.** How did the Israelites wandering in the desert for 40 years work logistically?

Numbers 1:46 states there were 603,550 men above the age of 20; if the Israelites did truly wander, how were necessities like sanitation, and housing handled?

**A.** For the entire 40 years, God was with them, and guiding them. The bible says He provided all their needs and they lacked for nothing.

> 12 Moreover thou leddest them in the day by a cloudy pillar; and in the night by a pillar of fire, to give them light in the way wherein they should go. 13 Thou camest down also upon mount Sinai, and spakest with them from heaven, and gavest them right judgments, and true laws, good statutes and commandments: 14 And madest known unto them thy holy sabbath, and commandedst them precepts, statutes, and laws, by the hand of Moses thy servant: 15 And gavest them

bread from heaven for their hunger, and broughtest forth water for them out of the rock for their thirst, and promisedst them that they should go in to possess the land which thou hadst sworn to give them (Nehemiah 9:12-15).

God was merciful even after they sinned against Him and began worshipping an idol they had made.

16 But they and our fathers dealt proudly, and hardened their necks, and hearkened not to thy commandments, And refused to obey, neither were mindful of thy wonders that thou didst among them; but hardened their necks, and in their rebellion appointed a captain to return to their bondage: but thou *art* a God ready to pardon, gracious and merciful, slow to anger, and of great kindness, and forsookest them not. 18 Yea, when they had made them a molten calf, and said, This *is* thy God that brought thee up out of Egypt, and had wrought great provocations; 19 Yet thou in thy manifold mercies forsookest them not in the wilderness: the pillar of the cloud departed not from them by day, to lead them in the way; neither the pillar of fire by night, to shew them light, and the way wherein they should go (Nehemiah 9:16-19).

He guided them, fed them and provided water for them. He prevented their clothes from wearing out. Although it does not actually say it, the children's clothes may have actually grown with them.

20 Thou gavest also thy good spirit to instruct them, and withheldest not thy manna from their mouth, and gavest them water for their thirst. 21 Yea, forty years didst thou sustain them in the wilderness, *so that* they

lacked nothing; their clothes waxed not old, and their feet swelled not (Nehemiah 9:20-21).

He gave them victory over all their enemies.

> 22 Moreover thou gavest them kingdoms and nations, and didst divide them into corners: so they possessed the land of Sihon, and the land of the king of Heshbon, and the land of Og king of Bashan (Nehemiah 9:22).

During all of this, the people grew in number until God led them into the Promised Land.

> 23 Their children also multipliedst thou as the stars of heaven, and broughtest them into the land, concerning which thou hadst promised to their fathers, that they should go in to possess *it* (Nehemiah 9:23).

With God, all things are possible (Mathew 19:26, Mark 9:23, 10:27, 14:36).

~~~

**Q.** Why didn't God deal with Adam and Eve's sin in the beginning and save us all this suffering?

**A.** It has been said that Adam could have been the sacrifice for Eve if he had refused to partake of the forbidden fruit.

What we read in Genesis sounds like what they did should not have been any big deal. But, once sin entered into the heart of humanity it not only began destroying Adam and Eve, it also put a curse on everything God had put under their dominion. The bible says that, "the gifts and calling of God *are* without repentance" (Romans 11:29).

What that means is that once the Lord decreed that Man would have dominion over all the Earth, He could not take it back. When Adam sinned, he reassigned his authority to the "person of sin."

The good news is that God had a plan that would redeem humanity by first becoming a man himself obeying and fulfilling the Law perfectly then becoming the everlasting payment for sin to anyone who believes in Him. We are promised that what we suffer in this life is nothing compared to the Joy we will have in eternity.

~~~

**Q.** Did Adam and Eve have children who practiced incest to create children to populate the earth?

**A.** Yes, but because Adam and Eve were genetically perfect the first few generations of humanity were not subject to the deformities that would be associated to incest today. As sin began to become more and more rampant in the Earth then genetic defects began to also degenerate humans. This is why incest is so dangerous today.

~~~

**Q.** Were Adam and Eve genetically identical?

I read in Genesis that eve was made from one of Adams ribs.

**A.** The short answer, mostly.

How do Christians address the possibility of genetic similarity between Adam and Eve?

The Genesis story is a beautiful tale of God's goodness and power. Everything God does is good. When He puts it all together, He says it is very good. Then God said it was not good for man to be alone. So, He takes Adam, shows him every living animal, and allows Adam to name each one. It shows that Adam himself was also creative to come up with a unique name for each animal he encountered. However, in all of Creation there was not a woman to be his companion. I think the point here is that God wanted Adam to know that it was He who had made all things and that before He gave Adam a companion, that he would realize that he needed to have a relationship with His Maker. Still the very first recorded words of Adam are "This *is* now bone of my bones, and flesh of my flesh: she shall be called Woman, because she was taken out of Man. Therefore shall a man leave his father and his mother, and shall cleave unto his wife: and they shall be one flesh." (Genesis 2:23-24)

Because Adam and Eve were genetically perfect, there would not have been any of the usual problems associated with inbreeding. Also, since they lived a flawless/sinless body they had no diseases. They had also been given authority over any problems. The world as we know it today happened after the fall of man and he was removed from the Garden of Eden. Today we face the problems Adam should have overcame.

~~~

**Q.** What do religious texts specify as the reason for Bathsheba to give into King David's seduction?

I was watching this documentary about King David's life and it mentioned that he seduced his soldier's wife. The wife of the solider, Bathsheba, tells him that she's loyal to her husband but after repeated seduction by David she gives in and becomes pregnant.

The stories always say how it was wrong and all but what was her reason to give in to it if she truly was loyal to her husband? I figure because he was perhaps focused more on duty as a solider than being her husband and she perhaps felt being loyal to him because she wanted to be honorable until she met David who adored her?

I also think that since it was a different time back then where people respected every command of the King and perhaps that's why she gave in?

**A.** To my knowledge, there is nothing in the Bible explaining Bathsheba's motives. The way the text reads is that David sent for her. She had no choice, but to obey the King, and come. She did have a choice as to whether or not she would sleep with him. He probably kept wooing her until she caved in. It is also possible that she opted for the bigger better deal. Being the King's wife or even his mistress may have seemed to be more beneficial to her, than the wife of a soldier. However, we do know that Bathsheba grieved for her Husband. "And when the wife of Uriah heard that Uriah her husband was dead, she mourned for her husband" (2Samuel 11:26).

We read very little about being devoted to a wife or husband out of love in the Old Testament. The few examples are with the patriarchs themselves. Abraham and Sarah, Jacob and Rachel but even then there was a lack of what looks like true devotion and respect for the wife. It is not until we get to the New Testament that we get a clear picture of a man devoted to one wife, and loving her as Christ loves the church.

~~~

**Q.** Will the Rapture help restore ecological balance to the Earth?

It seems that that many Christians leaving for life among the stars would greatly reduce the pressures on the planet, but perhaps I'm overestimating the effect this rather odd form of population control would have, or how long it would take before some other group of the "left behind" would simply fill the gap.

**A.** No, in fact the Bible says that after the rapture, the Apocalypse will occur the Sun and Moon will be 1/3 darker. Fire and Brimstone will fall from heaven, like a meteor shower.

> Likewise also as it was in the days of Lot; they did eat, they drank, they bought, they sold, they planted, they builded; But the same day that Lot went out of Sodom it rained fire and brimstone from heaven, and destroyed them all. Even thus shall it be in the day when the Son of man is revealed (Luke 17:28-30).

Because Lot was carried out of that city Christians have a picture of the Rapture, which will occur after the tribulation and before the Apocalypse.

> Immediately after the tribulation of those days shall the sun be darkened, and the moon shall not give her light, and the stars shall fall from heaven, and the powers of the heavens shall be shaken: (Mathew 24:29).

ⁿⁿⁿ

**Q.** What does God have to say about technology?

**A.** He takes credit for it, "I wisdom dwell with prudence, and find out knowledge of witty inventions" (Proverbs 8:12).

I am assuming you are asking if God has a problem with technology. I believe He gives us knowledge to advance our selves, although He is not always pleased with how we use these gifts. Technology falls under the "mammon of unrighteousness." Which means we can become attached to it and even worship it. If we use it wisely as good and proper stewards then Christians can expect to receive a good steward's reward. Jesus says that if you are not faithful in the unrighteous mammon then who will entrust us with the true riches (Luke 16:11).

I think one of the reasons He has allowed us to advance so far is because as we approach the "Last Days," we can use technology to help spread the Gospel. Nevertheless, the greater the technology the more the enemy can use it for his agenda. Therefore, I believe that before the end comes we will have a great revival, complete with miracles and Christians will pretty much abandon a lot of the high tech stuff. The Holy Spirit will have such a very strong presence, and we will not need it. This will be the final curtain call and will reach everyone on the planet. If you accept Jesus will be called up and those who reject Him will be left behind.

~~~

**Q.** How can you prove that Jesus really died on the cross and came back to life three days later?

**A.** There is no scientific proof. All we have are the testimonies of the witnesses. If you believe those testimonies, and the testimonies of those who have put their faith in Him, especially those recorded in the Bible, then put your faith in Jesus and He will prove Himself.

There has been a lot of discussion about Jesus, His existence and the record of His crucifixion. Those things are generally not debated. His resurrection and His divine purpose are what non-believers have issues with. All I can tell you is if you are unsure then search the Bible with a humble heart. If you believe there is a God at all, then ask Him to reveal himself.

Do whatever it takes; your eternal life is what is at stake. Not so much your temporal life that in the "grand scheme" of things is unimportant if there is no God, but is extremely valuable to a living God who was willing to die for you.

> Jesus said; The kingdom of heaven is like unto treasure hid in a field; the which when a man hath found, he hideth, and for joy thereof goeth and selleth all that he hath, and buyeth that field.

> Again; the kingdom of heaven is like unto a merchant man, seeking goodly pearls: Who, when he had found one pearl of great price, went and sold all that he had, and bought it (Mathew 13:44-46).

Now allow me to write to you the interpretation that the Lord taught me.

> The Kingdom of Heaven is humanity that has been lost in the world; but when Jesus came and found us He was so happy, that He gave up all that He had so he could purchase the world, with the people in it.

> Again; the Kingdom of Heaven is while God was searching the world seeking for humans to save and then he found you so He gave up his deity to become a

man then gave up his whole life to purchase you from
the sin of the world (Mathew 13:44-46, paraphrased).

The idea is that you are lost but Jesus is seeking for you and you are
more valuable to Him than you are to anyone in this world. He offers
eternal life in exchange for your temporary one.

~~~

# Chapter 8

# Other Religions

*"When we compare biblical Christianity with the religions of the world, using the Scriptures to guide us, we see that the gap between them is unbridgeable. In fact, one is forced to the conclusion that there are really only two religions in the world: biblical Christianity--and all other religions."* T.A. McMahon

1. What is the situation like for Christians in Pakistan?
2. Is Islam a religion that somehow makes its followers the most violent people on earth?
3. Does the Bible allow for Karma?
4. Given that religion is completely based on faith, why do theologians spend time on proving God's existence?
5. How can you rationalize millions of gods into just one Judeo Christian God or one "trinity" of Gods?
6. Is burning the Quran the same as burning a Bible?
7. What do the religious texts of Judaism, Christianity, and Islam have in common?
8. Is the Bible a copycat?
9. Let me propose something I call ***The Outsider Test***: If you were born in Saudi Arabia, you would be a Muslim right now, say it isn't so?
10. Why did humans create god?
11. What is the connection between Prometheus and Methuselah?

**Q.** What is the situation like for Christians in Pakistan?

**A.** Sometimes people ask questions that I cannot answer because I would have to have real life experience of the situation. This question was answered by Hasib Nazir, a Muslim on quora. com. It truly touched me so, with Nazir's permission, I thought I would include it. The photo is a screen shot from a televised Pakistani News show.

> I live in the village of Lahore. The majority of the population is Muslim and there are also some Christian's living in my village. You can call it a 95%-5% ratio. There has never been an incident of fighting between us; we are all living like brothers. They respect us and we respect them. There is also a church in my village where Christians worship every Sunday. We work together, we live together.
>
> This is just the small picture and the bigger picture also represents same thing. I often go to Lahore and I see great respect for Christians, we love each other.
>
> I also want to share a recent news story, "LAHORE: The Muslim and Christian communities came together during Sunday mass in a show of solidarity in Lahore" in a show of solidarity with the victims of a recent attack on the Peshawar church which resulted in over 100 deaths.
>
> So except for some extremists, all Pakistanis love Christians because we are Pakistanis first and we love every Pakistani whether they are Christian, Hindu or Singh.

There are several photos on the tribune web address,

http://tribune.com.pk/story/614333/muslims-form-human-chain-to-protect-christians-during-lahore-mass/

According to the article Muslims and Christians are holding up signs. Many in English declaring "One Nation; One Blood", "Many Faiths; One God", "No More Dialog; Only Action." Other signs were written in other languages but I imagine they had a similar message. A link to the incident that prompted the show of solidarity can be found in the accompanying article.

During my correspondence with Mr. Nazir I noticed that he felt a kinship with Christians and held them in high regard. This also seems to be the general feeling of most Muslims in Pakistan. It is not the average Muslim, who really wants to live peaceably, who needs to be feared as a terrorist. But, as Mr. Nazir pointed out, "except for the extremists."

~~~

**Q.** Is Islam a religion that somehow makes its followers the most violent people on earth?

**A.** I am not an expert on Islam, but one of the doctrines of the religion is the "Jihad *(Holy War)*." This can be similar to what Christians call the "war against the flesh" or it can be a violent war against any enemy of the religion itself and I suppose it can be interpreted either way, depending on which verse in the Quran is being quoted. If an Islamic leader of the religion wants a war against an enemy, they stir up followers with promises of heavenly rewards.

According to some hadith, if you are a martyr in a Jihad you will escape hell completely, be rewarded with 72 virgins, wine and all sorts of sensual pleasures that are denied while on Earth. *(A hadith is a writing used to interpret the Quran or establish laws and jurisprudence in Islamic nations. Hadiths are not considered holy and are often debated among Islamic clerics.)*

The religion has an aggressive agenda with a long history of hostilities towards Judaism and Christianity as well as other Eastern religions. They believe the whole world will eventually convert to Islam or be annihilated. Islam does not force conversions, however; those who do not convert are considered infidels. Hadiths number into the thousands and are often contradictory. Depending on the hadith, Christians are allowed to repent and convert to the religion. Non-believers are to become servants under Sharia Law. In addition, anyone caught worshipping any other God can be put to death.

I have written this answer in part from research and in part from my memories of discussions with Muslims who lived in the US. Some were co-workers trying to convert me others were employers who were reluctant to share their beliefs. I do not claim to have studied this religion or understand it.

~~~

**Q.** Does the Bible allow for Karma?

Over and over again, the Bible mentions suffering or consequences for people's sinful actions, such as the experiences of King Saul, David and others, who suffered later for their sinful actions. Even Jesus says "God Please Forgive their Sins".

Does this mean the Bible allows for the concept of "Karma"?

Karma in Indian religions is the concept of "action" or "deed", understood as that which causes the entire cycle of cause and effect. (wikipedia.com)

**A.** The Closest thing Christianity comes to Karma is; "Be not deceived, God is not mocked, whatsoever a man soweth that shall he also reap" (Galatians 6:7). Generally, we believe that even if you are "Born Again" you are not free to treat God's grace as a cloak to commit sin and live the same way you have. When a person repents, it is a lifelong work to gain deeper and deeper knowledge of the things of Christ. Now let us get a better definition of Karma.

> Karma: noun—In Indian philosophy, the influence of an individual's past actions on his future lives or reincarnations. It is based on the conviction that the present life is only one in a chain of lives (*see* samsara). The accumulated moral energy of a person's life determines his or her character, class status, and disposition in the next life. The process is automatic, and no interference by the gods is possible. In the course of a chain of lives, people can perfect themselves and reach the level of Brahma, or they can degrade themselves to the extent that they return to life as animals. The concept of karma, basic to Hinduism, was also incorporated into Buddhism and Jainism. *(Concise Encyclopedia)*

Karma then, as I understand the concept works over several reincarnations of a soul and each new life is a result of how well you lived the last one. Christianity does not believe in reincarnation, the bible makes it plain that, "~It is appointed unto men once to die, but after this the judgment:" (Hebrews 9:27).

The goal of Eastern Pantheist doctrine of karma is to reach nirvana by making each succession life better than the previous life, until you have accumulated enough enlightenment to be allowed to rejoin the Brahma or universal spirit.

God's goal through Christ is to redeem humanity. Christians believe that because God loves humanity so much that He desires to have a relationship with us. He offers to fill us with His Spirit, not because we have done anything towards earning it but because He is a gracious God who forgives our sins, when we turn away from them and believe in Jesus.

Pantheism's karma says you must earn paradise and if you do worse you could go through a few thousand years being at the bottom of the food chain or worse a flea bitten dog. Christianity offers free salvation and eternal life all you have to do is ask Jesus to come into your life and believe that God raised Him from the dead. All your sin is washed away and if you sin after wards God will continue to work in you and lead you back to Him. You may lose something in the judgment but you will still be saved.

~~~

**Q.** Given that religion is completely based on faith, why do theologians spend time on proving God's existence?

**A.** The only proof of God's existence is when God himself, reveals himself. I do not think most theologians are trying to prove God's existence in science, but are working to show that science cannot disprove God's existence.

The true believer is not living by blind faith; our reassurance is in the heart. Unbelievers attack our faith laugh at us and think we are somehow less intelligent or do not have enough education to dispel our beliefs.

Of course faith does leave the door open for charlatans, that fake some miracle or deceive people with a lot of smooth talk or point to some worldly disaster and come up with some convoluted story that

God has brought judgment because the area was so evil. The whole world is evil in His sight and He will judge it when it is time. Until then, please know that the Earth is in rebellion against sin, which causes these natural disasters.

If you want to know God, then do not look at what is happening in the world and instead search His word, believe that it is true and ask the Lord to guide you to the truth of whom He is. He seeks for you to know Him personally and He wants to tell you things but He said much of what He wants to tell you, you are not ready to receive.

~~~

**Q.** How can you rationalize millions of gods into just one Judeo Christian God or one "trinity" of Gods?

If you believe that one god exists then you must concede that millions of gods can exist.

**A.** Sure I believe that there are millions of deities, some are worshiped because they are liars and have conned followers into worshiping them, but most of these modern worshipers do not even recognize they are worshiping a false god. In fact most of the false gods today are the gods of self, or money, or if not money then the power of money. Essentially, whatever a person dedicates their life to pursue can become their god.

However, I perceive that you are probably asking about the ancient pagan gods, which once wielded so much power over the lives of people. They are still around, but they are hiding behind a whole new set of lies. God recognizes their existence, but He has given humanity free will so He now waits until the time when no one else will turn away from the liars and come to the knowledge of Jesus.

Jesus is patient and longsuffering, so that as long as there is a chance to save one more person then the one who searches the hearts of all men waits. In the end, He will save the ones who come to Him and destroy those who refused His salvation.

~~~

**Q.** Is burning the Quran the same as burning a Bible?

Is there a cultural significance that magnifies the impact?

**A.** For a Muslim the Quran is considered extremely Holy, especially if it is written in its original Arabic language. The translations are not so much, but still great care is taken in how the book is handled. When a copy is worn-out it is supposed to be burned or placed in a tomb where it could never be stepped on. For much of its history, it was not allowed to be handled except by a Muslim clergyman and he had to go through a ritual bath before he could open it.

When I worked for a Muslim family, they kept a copy of the Quran taped to their cash register. It was still in the box it was purchased in and looked real bad, with the tape collecting grease and dust. They ran a cafeteria-style restaurant and the register was at the end of the line and looked terrible, so I decided I would clean up. As soon as I got close to the Quran, they stopped me and told me I was not allowed to touch it. At the time, I had no idea what the Quran was and had very little knowledge of the religion.

Out of respect for their beliefs, I never bothered it again but I never could understand the reverence they gave a book, or the belief that it protected the money in the register. At the time, it seemed more like idolatry. Since then I have learned to see the importance of protecting the integrity of certain writings, especially with so many

English translations of the Bible, which can change the meaning of entire passages. It is also, why our government takes such precautions with the constitution of the US. However, this went beyond that, because they were not even allowed to touch a copy of it unless they were clean. For the most part, they could not read it as I do my Bible.

These were decent people who treated me fairly, but could not tell me much about their beliefs. They seemed genuinely surprised that I knew so much and understood so much about the Old Testament prophets. They truly loved to hear me talk about Jesus and I thought at the time that they did not know about Him. They actually reverenced Jesus but only as a prophet. They did not get the whole Lion and Lamb analogy and they thought that because I could read the Bible without going through any special ritual that the book itself was unclean.

Getting back to the question, burning either book in an act of malice or contempt Muslims would regard it to be punishable and in some of the strictest sects, defacing a Quran could be punishable by death. In a strict Christian society, burning a Bible might be sacrilege and shameful, but not punishable. While burning a Quran would not be of any significance because it is regarded as a false doctrine.

~~~

**Q.** What do the religious texts of Judaism, Christianity, and Islam have in common?

**A.** All three have very similar teachings from Genesis 1:1 through Genesis 21, when Sari sends Hagar and Ishmael away. This would include the creation story, the fall of Adam and Eve, Noah's Ark, when God calls Abram, and when God change his name, from Abram to Abraham. After Sarah sends Hagar and Ishmael away, the Quran begins to follow the life and descendants of Ishmael. Whom they claim is the righteous seed of Abraham and the forefather of Muhammad. Still they recognize the stories of Sodom and Gomorrah, Moses as the lawgiver, and the plagues and miracles of ancient Egypt during the exodus. All three recognize most if not all of the prophets in the Old Testament especially the Psalms and Proverbs.

Neither Jews nor Christians recognize Muhammad as a prophet. Neither Jews nor Muslims recognize the New Testament claims that Jesus is the Son of God, and generally dismiss most or all of the New Testament as God's word.

Some Jews do not believe that Jesus ever existed or if He did, He is at most a prophet. Some even say he was a charlatan.

Muslims believe Jesus or *(Isa)* was a prophet and is the slave of Allah, but not the Son of God, nor the redeemer.

Christians believe that Jesus is the Messiah promised by God throughout the Old Testament prophets. Muslims claim some of those prophesies point to Muhammad, and Jews claim that the Messiah has not yet come.

~~~

**Q.** Is the Bible a copycat?

I started hearing a lot about the Bible being a copycat story of Horus and with similarities to Mithras. Is this true?

Horus is an Egyptian god who lived 3000 years before the formation of Christianity.

**A.** This sounds like neo *(modern)* paganism's attempt to confuse and debunk the truth of God's word with ancient mythology.

The New Testament was written in the first century largely by the disciples, and Apostles, or their assistants. Christianity at that time was very pure and holy. The Apostles were so filled with the Holy Spirit that when they traveled to foreign lands, where pagan religions were being practiced, that the people fell under such conviction that they willing destroyed their own books of spells and incantations, and sought the forgiveness of God through Jesus Christ. The new faith had no special rituals or holidays, to try to garner favor with the gods of paganism. Repentance meant to leave those things behind and live a new life in Christ being filled with and led by His Spirit.

As Christianity began to spread, it did so under great persecution. Those who did not convert appealed to the governors, most of whom were also pagans, accusing the followers of Christianity of desecrating their holy places. Being a Christian was not a popular choice, but for a believer it was better to be accepted by God, and hated by men, even if it meant dying a horrible death. Yes, pagans would torture and kill Christians. According to the first century historian, Tacticus, Caesar Nero would burn Christians to light his Garden at night.

> ~ Nero fastened the guilt and inflicted the most exquisite tortures on a class hated for their abominations, called Christians by the populace. Christus, from whom the name had its origin, suffered the extreme penalty during the reign of Tiberius at the hands of one of our procurators, Pontius Pilatus, and a most mischievous superstition, thus checked for the moment, again broke out not only in Judæa, the first source of the evil, but even in Rome, where all things hideous and shameful from every part of the world find their centre and become popular. Accordingly, an arrest was first made of all who pleaded guilty; then, upon their information, an immense multitude was convicted, not so much of the crime of firing the city, as of hatred against

mankind. Mockery of every sort was added to their deaths. Covered with the skins of beasts, they were torn by dogs and perished, or were nailed to crosses, or were doomed to the flames and burnt, to serve as a nightly illumination, when daylight had expired. (Translated from Tacitus from his published work *Annals* 15.44 *(circa 117AD)*, in the second Medicean manuscript)

Persecutions like that continued until Emperor Constantine's reign in the fourth century. At which time, in order to keep peace between Christians and pagans Constantine merged many of the pagan holidays with the events concerning Christ in the Bible. You can research "Constantine I and Christianity," if you want to know more.

As Christianity spread, the world simultaneously entered into the dark ages. Not because of the spread of Christianity, but because rather than making true converts, and abandoning pagan rituals, they polluted the Gospel with these holidays and traditions, something that God does not approve of. Our modern Christian traditions celebrate things like Christmas on Dec. 25, because that was a date that many pagans already celebrated their deity.

The claims that Horus or any other mythological god was born of a virgin, died, and rose again, were ever believed by Egyptians 5000 years ago is unlikely. The founders of Christian faith were all devout Jews, who knew and believed in the Old Testament. They would not have borrowed anything from pagan beliefs, nor did they need to. The Old Testament provides evidence that a Messiah was supposed to come from the genealogy of Judah and King David. Jesus' life and crucifixion is generally not disputed among most historians, and scholars that have studied the period, even from a secular position. Most people accept the probability that Jesus was an actual historical figure, given the grand scale of witnesses and testimonies attributed to Jesus as a person.

The bulk of the evidence of Jesus having actually lived is the Bible, and the high improbability that stories of Him would have just been made up by the Church fathers, who were highly persecuted for believing, and spreading them. In other words the Apostles had more to lose than to gain, by spreading the story of His life, and resurrection, to have just made up a fictitious figure. Because of that, many secular historians and atheists agree; the church fathers knew Him personally and were convinced that He arose from death. That statement does not require them to believe that Jesus is God, but a man who was executed and His followers for whatever reasons continued to spread His teachings.

~~~

**Q.** Let me propose something I call *The Outsider Test*: If you were born in Saudi Arabia, you would be a Muslim right now, say it isn't so?

That is a cold hard fact. Dare you deny it? Since this is so, or at least 99% so, then the proper method to evaluate your religious beliefs is with a healthy measure of skepticism. **Test your beliefs as if you were an outsider to the faith you are evaluating**. If your faith stands up under muster, then you can have your faith. If not, abandon it, for **any God who requires you to believe correctly when we have this extremely strong tendency to believe what we were born into, surely should make the correct faith pass the outsider test. If your faith cannot do this, then the God of your faith is not worthy of being worshipped.**

**A.** I have talked to a lot of people from Muslim nations that became atheist or agnostics, after they were able to get away from the influence of their governments. So my answer is, "I don't know." That is why I want to reach the Muslim population with the

Gospel. Most people believe in God, even if they do not believe in the dogma of religion. People recognize it is a personal choice that should never be forced. This is why the inquisitions were so brutal, because rational people who believed in God did not believe the state religions' interpolation of the gospel, which seemed only to serve the state and the church. Not the people as Christ taught.

As for me personally I was not raised in a religious family. Although I was shipped off to a church every Sunday. It was mostly because my Father worked on Sundays, and my step mother wanted a break from having his kids *(there were four of us)* around. The Church bus would come through every Sunday pick us up and return us that afternoon. What I got from that experience really didn't amount to much. Sunday school was ok, but mostly consisted of bible stories from the Old Testament. There was very little talk about how much God loves us or how to have a relationship with the Lord. If you asked too many probing questions, you were told that those kinds of questions came from the devil and should not be asked. If something did not fit their little theological box, then they changed the subject. Most of them were nice people, but as I look back on the experience, it didn't appear to have much influence over any decisions I ever made towards God. The main service consisted of an angry pastor, railing about sin and how angry God was. Sunday after Sunday he preached about hell, and how you needed to be ready to meet God. Then there was the alter call, and people were asked to come forward so they could be saved. It seemed to me that the same people went forward every week. I think they went up to pray about various troubles or perhaps for family members they wanted to get saved.

I have shared my own personal journey in various other questions of this book. This was a very traditional church. While I will not say that it did not have some impact on my life. I will say that when I was old enough to be on my own, I had no desire to go to church, and have some pastor lay a guilt trip on me.

~~~

**Q.** Why did humans create god?

**A.** Because, they believe the true God hates them. Therefore, they create gods they can control. The problem is they cannot really control them; they however will try to control them.

~~~

**Q.** What is the connection between Prometheus and Methuselah?

The two names share an apparent common root in -meth- with -selah and pro- being common additions.

I am curious about whatever connection there might be between these two.

**A.** In the Greek Mathusala came from the Hebrew word Methuselah and is considered one of the predelugian *(pre-flood)* patriarchs. Methuselah is the son of Enoch who walked with God. When traced back his name could be interpreted as a Man sent forth as a spear. He was the longest living individual spoken of in the Old Testament.

I will be using a Strong's Lexicon to trace these words

**G3103**
Μαθουσάλα
Mathousala
*math-oo-sal'-ah*

Of Hebrew origin [H4968]; *Mathusala* (that is, *Methushelach*), an antediluvian: - Mathusala.

### H4968

מתושלח

mᵉthûshelach

*meth-oo-sheh'-lakh*

From H4962 and H7973; *man of a dart*; *Methushelach*, an antediluvian patriarch: - Methuselah.

The Hebrew Name is a compound word using "meth" or "math H4962," which means Adult male which will live the full length, and "selah H5542" or "shelack H7973" which means to propel.

### H4962

מת

math

*math*

From the same as H4970; properly an *adult* (as of full length); by implication a *man* (only in the plural): - + few, X friends, men, persons, X small.

The second half of the name is selah H5542 or shelack H7973, which means to propel forward as an attack with a spear. So if Methuselah lived up to his name, then it could very well mean that He lived till the Great Flood as a man sent forth against evil. Many of the Psalms of David incorporate the word selah in them so, if you look at this in the light of the New Testament, one could make the case that Methuselah was involved in Spiritual Warfare.

### H7973

שלח

shelach

*sheh'-lakh*

From H7971; a *missile* of attack, that is, *spear*; also (figuratively) a *shoot* of growth, that is, *branch:* - dart, plant, X put off, sword, weapon.

**H5542**
סלה
selâh
*seh'-law*
From H5541; *suspension* (of music), that is, *pause:* - Selah.

Since the Strong's Lexicon is mainly limited to words found in the KJV Bible, finding a definition for a Greek "meth" was not as clear. The words containing it generally associated it with *methodeia* a "traveling trickster," *methusos,* a "drunkard," and *methorios,* "an associate of" or "tied to something." It did seem that "meth" in both languages are translated as "man" in English, with the suffixes or prefixes attached to represent the condition of the man i.e. prankster, drunkard, associate, etc.

"ProG4253" clearly means "something from before" and appears to be a prefix that translates to the English prefix "pre." The suffix, "eus G2095" directly translates to "good." So "Prometheus" can literally be translated to "Premangood." This could describe much of the mythology concerning Prometheus. According to the myth, he is supposed to have been man's creator and benefactor for giving man fire. He was tied to a rock where an eagle ate his liver everyday as punishment for stealing fire from the gods and giving it to man. He also has an association with Pandora. If these myths are traceable to pre-Noah's flood then Prometheus would have been one of the Nephilim or fallen Giants, spoken of in Genesis 6. Of course, that is just speculation and will have to remain such unless some real evidence could confirm it. If this was indeed the case, then Methuselah and Prometheus would have been on opposite sides of good and evil.

It is also interesting that when Aaron's sons tried to bring strange fire before the Alter of God, that the FIRE OF GOD went out from God and devoured them. This would indicate that the fire of Prometheus is defiantly not acceptable to the Holy Fire of GOD. (Leviticus 9:23-10:4)

~~~

# Chapter 9

# Spiritual Gifts and the Supernatural

*"I used to think that God's gifts were on shelves one above the other and that the taller we grow in Christian character the more easily we could reach them. I now find that God's gifts are on shelves one beneath the other and that it is not a question of growing taller but of stooping lower." F.B. Meyer*

1. Do you believe in miracles?
2. What does it feel like to speak in tongues?
3. If I do not speak in tongues, does that mean I am not baptized in the Holy Spirit?
4. Is lucid dreaming biblical?
5. How can I have a spiritual or supernatural experience with God?

**Q.** Do you believe in miracles?

**A.** Yes, I do believe in miracles and was once a vessel of God that performed one.

Although I had accepted Christ as a child, I had been taught that miracles had "ceased" when the New Testament was completed. By the time, I was a young adult I had fallen away from church and although I still believed in God, I felt like I was pretty much on my own until one day I heard someone talking about "FAITH." It was the way he said the word that shot an arrow straight to my heart. I began seeking God with fervor after that, studying my Bible diligently. One day I threw up my hands to God and said, "Lord, I can't understand this. It is too complicated, who is right; the Mormons, the Catholics, the Baptists, the Muslims? How can a man know who is right and who is wrong? Are they all saying the same things?

Finally, I got bold and cried out, "Lord, the one who created all things from the beginning; I am calling on YOU right now to show me the way. If I wind up in hell when I die, it is because YOU did not save me when I asked." He heard me and almost immediately after that He began showing me scriptures and giving me understanding. He taught me how to pray both in the spirit and in my understanding.

Then one day after He had led me to a Church; I was praying and one of the women was trying to comfort a baby. I do not think he was more than a few months old at the time. He was crying, and nothing would calm him. While praying internally I reached my hand, touched the back of the child's head, and said, "Help him Lord." The child stopped immediately and looked straight at me. When I touched him, I felt a surge or something flow through me.

Now it did not stop there, that little boy had been sent to Church on a bus, when he was taken home the anointing that had flowed through me to him also touched the boy's parents. Within a month or so, they started attending Church and received Jesus Christ as their Lord and Savior. They never knew who it was that had touched their child but they knew he had been touched and loved and reached. I should mention here that the reason the child was crying was because he was autistic. No one knew it at the time but God; he was just a little boy that was brought in on a bus. Over the years, that little boy and I became buddies.

~~~

Q. What does it feel like to speak in tongues?

A. I received the Gift of tongues sometime in the 1990's, after I had begun a spiritual journey to understand who God is and which of the many religions are true.

I feel I should share a little of that journey with you here. At that time, I was being pulled in several directions at once. I had one "christian" tell me that tongues were ceased and others told me I had to be baptized a certain way. I wondered about the Mormons, the Catholics, the Baptists, the Muslims, the New Age theism. I even thought about becoming Amish or Mennonite. All of whom were telling me different paths to God. My head was amassed with confusion and doctrines. I had heard of Pentecostals, but what I heard was they were crazy, or some sort of cult. I really did not know anything about nor was I particularly interested in speaking in tongues.

What I did to make sense out of the chaos, was to go on what I now call a 'Media Fast.' I avoided television, radios, newspapers and even family and friends. I only communicated enough to be polite and would quickly excuse myself and depart. At work I had to deal with clients, I was an HVAC tech at the time, so I could not completely escape having to hear things that the client may have on in their homes. Once I knew what the problem was I focused doing the repairs keeping my thoughts off anything else. Then in my spare time, I read my Bible. I bought one without any study notes and with large clear print so I could read it without getting fatigued. I remember getting to the passage where...

> In Gibeon the LORD appeared to Solomon in a dream by night: and God said, Ask what I shall give thee.
>
> And Solomon said, Thou hast shewed unto thy servant David my father great mercy, according as he walked before thee in truth, and in righteousness, and in uprightness of heart with thee; and thou hast kept for him this great kindness, that thou hast given him a son to sit on his throne, as it is this day. And now, O LORD my God, thou hast made thy servant king instead of David my father: and I am but a little child: I know not how to go out or come in. And thy servant is in the midst of thy people which thou hast chosen, a great people, that cannot be numbered nor counted for multitude. Give therefore thy servant an understanding heart to judge thy people, that I may discern between good and bad: for who is able to judge this thy so great a people?
>
> 10 And the speech pleased the Lord, that Solomon had asked this thing (1Kings 3:5-10).

As soon as I read that, I was compelled to fall on my face before God and say...

> "Lord you have given me this life and I am but a child. I do not know which way I should go I cannot discern what is right, and what is evil, for you alone know all, and see all. I place my soul's salvation in your care.

Therefore, let it be that if I should end up in hell then it is not my fault. This is the record of a man who put his whole life before you and if you are truly God then you will hear my cry. Deliver me from my ignorance, and show me the life you purposed for me. If I should be nothing in this life, then let me not be a stumbling block to others, and if I am to be like Solomon to teach wisdom and give good doctrine then it will have to be by your Spirit, and by your leading, for I can do nothing by myself."

It was not long after that the Lord began showing and revealing things from His Word to me that no one I had ever heard preach ever revealed. After several months, He led me through circumstance to a little Church that confirmed everything that He had begun showing me. It was there that I 1st heard about speaking in tongues. But, I am getting a little ahead of myself. During those months after my prayer, I would sometimes wake up at night, and sit straight up in the bed. I felt as though something in the pit of my gut would try to express itself. My jaws would begin moving and my tongue would cleave to the roof of my mouth. I knew this had to do with something from God, but I could not let it loose. Before long at my new Church, the Pastor taught about the gift of the "Baptism of the Holy Spirit." He then gave an invitation saying, "If anyone wanted to be baptized in the Spirit to come forward and have hands laid on you." I practically flew to the front of the Church. He laid his hands on me and prayed… at first, nothing happened but that night when my spirit woke me up I began to utter a very lyrical language that I could not understand. Since that time, I have pretty much been able to "Pray in Tongues" at will. I have never been given a prophetic tongue and interpretation. Neither have I been given an interpretation of another person's prophetic tongue. As for the experience it actually varies, sometimes I feel as though God is speaking through me, other times it is as though I am in a praise and worship service, with no one but the Lord and I. Still other times I feel a deep urgency to pray, as if God is using me to battle something in the Earth. At times, I think I am actually making supplications for foreign missionaries. However, I cannot say that with any certainty on my part, the Lord knows.

~~~

**Q.** If I do not speak in tongues, does that mean I am not baptized in the Holy Spirit?

What is the crux of the disagreement in scripture by doctrine between Christians?

**A.** No, it does not mean you are not baptized in the Holy Spirit. But, let's look at the Doctrine of Baptisms as the Scripture teaches us that this is a forward move in personal spiritual growth.

> Therefore leaving the principles of the doctrine of Christ, let us go on unto perfection; not laying again the foundation of repentance from dead works, and of faith toward God, **Of the doctrine of baptisms,** and of laying on of hands, and of resurrection of the dead, and of eternal judgment. And this will we do, if God permit (Hebrews 6:1-3).

The doctrine of the "Baptism of the Holy Spirit" (Mathew 3:11, Mark 1:8, Luke 3:16, Acts 8:14-17) was recognized during the Azusa Street Revival in 1906. Since then it has spread and like most things of God men have taken sound doctrine and rewrote it to suit them. One of the doctrines claims that if you do not have this gift you are not saved. The idea is that some people who have spoken in tongues use that as the evidence of their salvation. The Bible tells us that the righteous walk by faith. We see their faith by their good works and the evidence of salvation is the fruit of the spirit which is manifested as, "love, joy, peace, longsuffering, gentleness, goodness, faith, meekness and temperance~" (Galatians 5:22-23.) In short, salvation is by grace through faith, which is given to you, but the evidence of faith is the fruit of the spirit, which manifest as good works, not tongue talking.

Then you have the sect that says, "Tongues have ceased." This comes from misquoting a scripture in 1corinthians. The doctrine is that tongues ceased when the New Testament was completed.

> 8 Charity never faileth: but whether there be prophecies, they shall fail; whether there be tongues, they shall cease; whether there be knowledge, it shall vanish away. 9 For we know in part, and we prophesy in part. 10 But when that which is perfect is come, then that which is in part shall be done away (1Corinthians 13:8 -10).

Those who believe tongues have ceased quote the above passage but stop at the end of verse nine. What the passage really means is that what is being done in part now will be complete, when that which is perfect is come. The Holy Spirit is perfect and He brought His Gifts when He came. He is still here and will remain until the day of the harvest and Christians are raptured. The gifts of the Spirit including tongues will remain as long as the Holy Spirit is here. The perfection that Paul speaks about is after the "New Heaven" and "New Earth" are made, sin and all evil have been cast into the lake of fire. Until then the Holy Spirit is here to manifest itself however and whenever He chooses to guide us into all truth. How can anyone believe that perfection is complete when there is so much misinterpretation of scriptures?

The Baptism of the Holy Spirit is a separate work from salvation. Usually, it results in the baptized speaking in tongues but I have known Christians who after receiving the baptism have other gifts manifest but never spoke in any tongue other than their own. It is usually passed through a believer who has been baptized into the Holy Spirit when they lay hands on someone seeking to be baptized into the Holy Spirit.

The misunderstanding comes because when a person receives Jesus as their savior they are baptized into the Body of Christ. This baptism is the "ONE BAPTISM" that the scripture speaks of and all Christians must go through. Don't worry it is automatic the moment you confess Jesus as your Lord and believe in your heart that God raised Him from the dead you were baptized into the Body of Christ. And the same spirit which raised Christ from the dead dwells in you. Many Scriptures describe this as dying and being reborn a new creature.

Most Christians believe that after you are saved that you should be baptized in water. I think of this as a physical representation of a spiritual manifestation.

Now let us look back at Hebrews 6:1-3 again. He speaks of leaving behind the foundations of the doctrine of Christ so that you can move forward unto perfection. The "Doctrine of Baptisms" is one doctrine, but many baptisms all of them (Body of Christ, Holy Spirit and water) are a part of the Spiritual Growth to perfection. I will save the rest of the doctrines of laying on of hands, and of resurrection of the dead, and of eternal judgment for another question. However, they are part of that same growth, too.

～～～

**Q.** Is lucid dreaming biblical?

**A.** I would be digress in this teaching if I merely answered the questions as is without having you examine your dreams to see if they are just a rehash of a busy life. More importantly, if you are on some type of medication whose side effects cause dreams or hallucinations? Have you been diagnosed with some mental disorder such as Schizophrenia or Multiple Sclerosis, which have been known to cause such things?

If you are having these dreams then you need to recognize whether or not they are just dreams, or if they are indeed prophetic. I give you this advice; examine them closely and get to know the Lord personally, remain humble and study the Bible. God does speak to us through our dreams, but He also warns us about a spirit of delusion that deceives the boastful and defiant.

God tells us that dreams can come from a busy life.

> Be not rash with thy mouth, and let not thine heart be hasty to utter *any* thing before God: for God *is* in heaven, and thou upon earth: therefore let thy words be few. For a dream cometh through the multitude of business; and a fool's voice *is known* by multitude of words (Ecclesiastes 5:2-3)

He also tells us that some dreams are prophetic. Perhaps the best reference to a lucid dream in the Bible, is when Abram fell asleep, and God spoke to him. He said, "Know for sure" I think that covers the definition of lucid.

> And when the sun was going down, a deep sleep fell upon Abram; and, lo, an horror of great darkness fell upon him. And he said unto Abram, Know of a surety that thy seed shall be a stranger in a land that is not theirs, and shall serve them; and they shall afflict them four hundred years; And also that nation, whom they shall serve, will I judge: and afterward shall they come out with great

substance. And thou shalt go to thy fathers in peace; thou shalt be buried in a good old age. But in the fourth generation they shall come hither again: for the iniquity of the Amorites is not yet full (Genesis 15:12-16).

Many years later, the Lord told the Children of Israel, "Hear now my words: If there be a prophet among you, *I* the LORD will make myself known unto him in a vision, *and* will speak unto him in a dream" (Numbers 12:6).

Through His prophet Jeremiah, He tells us, "The prophet that hath a dream, let him tell a dream; and he that hath my word, let him speak my word faithfully. What *is* the chaff to the wheat? saith the LORD" (Jeremiah 23:28). Pay attention to the question the Lord put forth here. "What *is* the Chaff to the Wheat?"

Chaff is the protective husk or covering on a kernel of wheat. So what is given in a dream or prophesy is meant to help keep the prophesy safe until it is fulfilled. Once the Wheat is fully formed and harvested the chaff is separated and discarded. On a side note concerning chaff, in many ways religion is like the chaff on the truth. Many of the ordinances of the Old Testament were like chaff. Once Christ came and fulfilled the prophecies concerning Him up to that point, He discarded the chaff, i.e. it is no longer necessary to sacrifice animals to cover sins, or to hold to dietary laws, stoning, etc. In the same way, many of the Christian sects and religions have managed to protect God's word, but now we are coming of full age and ready for harvest. The religion is being threshed off and the truth is beginning to emerge. Once it does, the Bible says the "Sons of God" will manifest themselves in the Earth. There will be a great worldwide revival and then Jesus will return and gather the wheat into His barn.

My footnotes say, "What: That is, when the dreamers declare their dreams, and the true prophets faithfully declare their message, the difference between them will be as evident as that between the chaff and the wheat." I really don't agree with that because the lord tells us that prophesy, visions and dreams will return in the last days.

> And it shall come to pass afterward, that I will pour out my spirit upon all flesh; and your sons and your daughters shall prophesy, your old men shall dream dreams, your young men shall see visions: (Joel 2:28)

> And it shall come to pass in the last days, saith God, I will pour out of my Spirit upon all flesh: and your sons and your daughters shall prophesy, and your young men shall see visions, and your old men shall dream dreams: (Acts 2:17)

The Holy Spirit of God is not going to deceive you so any dream, vision, prophesy, gift, etc. that the Holy Spirit reveals should be received faithfully. So to answer your question, "Are *'lucid'* dreams biblical?" Based on all the scriptures I have shared; yes, but it is very important to know that not all dreams and visions are from God. Let's go back to Jeremiah and read the verses that surround 23:28 and specifically verses 25, 27 and 32.

> 25 I have heard what the prophets said, that prophesy lies in my name, saying, I have dreamed, I have dreamed. 26 How long shall *this* be in the heart of the prophets that prophesy lies? yea, *they are* prophets of the deceit of their own heart;

> 27 Which think to cause my people to forget my name by their dreams which they tell every man to his neighbour, as their fathers have forgotten my name for Baal. *(Note: Baal was a demon god of the Philistines*

*but the statement would hold true for any false dream, prophesy, teaching or doctrine.)*

28 The prophet that hath a dream, let him tell a dream; and he that hath my word, let him speak my word faithfully. What *is* the chaff to the wheat? saith the LORD. 29 *Is* not my word like as a fire? saith the LORD; and like a hammer *that* breaketh the rock in pieces?

30 Therefore, behold, I *am* against the prophets, saith the LORD, that steal my words every one from his neighbour. 31 Behold, I *am* against the prophets, saith the LORD, that use their tongues, and say, He saith. 32 Behold, I *am* against them that prophesy false dreams, saith the LORD, and do tell them, and cause my people to err by their lies, and by their lightness; yet I sent them not, nor commanded them: therefore they shall not profit this people at all, saith the LORD (Jeremiah 23:25-32).

Remember, I mentioned about a "spirit of delusion?" Well you will find that here,

*Even him,* whose coming is after the working of Satan with all power and signs and lying wonders, And with all deceivableness of unrighteousness in them that perish; because they received not the love of the truth, that they might be saved. And for this cause God shall send them strong delusion, that they should believe a lie: That they all might be damned who believed not the truth, but had pleasure in unrighteousness (2Thesalonians 2:9-12).

Beloved, believe not every spirit, but try the spirits whether they are of God: because many false prophets are gone out into the world.

> Hereby know ye the Spirit of God: Every spirit that
> confesseth that Jesus Christ is come in the flesh is of
> God: And every spirit that confesseth not that Jesus
> Christ is come in the flesh is not of God: and this is
> that *spirit* of antichrist, whereof ye have heard that it
> should come; and even now already is it in the world.

> Ye are of God, little children, and have overcome them:
> because greater is he that is in you, than he that is in
> the world. They are of the world: therefore speak they
> of the world, and the world heareth them (1John 4:1-5).

There are many other references to this, but these make it pretty clear. As I said if you believe God is giving you prophetic dreams, then get to know the "One True God; Jesus Christ," and His word and ask Him about them. God bless you for asking about this very important topic.

Be assured of this one thing that if you accept Jesus you can go to the Father through Him and if you ask for truth He will tell you the truth and He will make it plain *(lucid)* enough that you will know it is Him.

> Jesus said, Ask, and it shall be given you; seek, and ye
> shall find; knock, and it shall be opened unto you. For
> every one that asketh receiveth; and he that seeketh
> findeth; and to him that knocketh it shall be opened.
> If a son shall ask bread of any of you that is a father,
> will he give him a stone? or if *he ask* a fish, will he for
> a fish give him a serpent? Or if he shall ask an egg, will
> he offer him a scorpion? If ye then, being evil, know
> how to give good gifts unto your children: how much
> more shall *your* heavenly Father give the Holy Spirit
> to them that ask him? (Luke 11:9-13)

~~~

**Q.** How can I have a spiritual or supernatural experience with God?

How can I have an experience like?

- The Apostle Paul's vision;
- Jacob wrestling the angel;
- Moses and the Burning Bush;
- Isaiah and the vision of the Angels;
- Elijah and talks with God;
- (…)

**A.** You are asking for a pretty tall order. While God may very well give you such a visit or manifestation, I would ask would you be willing to accept what God does give you. *"To place ourselves in range of God's choicest gifts, we have to walk with God, work with God, lean on God, cling to God, come to have the sense and feel of God, refer all things to God."* (Cornelius Plantinga)

For most Christians they simply trust that God is "out there somewhere," but what you are asking for is a very real personal encounter with a Righteous, and Holy God. First let me give you some very practical advice, God is sovereign which means He makes the rules not you or me. He also keeps His promises and He does promise that he will be found of those who diligently seek Him.

Every one of these scriptures tells us He can be found.

> But if from thence thou shalt seek the LORD thy God, thou shalt find *him,* if thou _seek him_ with all thy heart and with all thy soul (Deuteronomy 4:29).

> And thou, Solomon my son, know thou the God of thy father, and serve him with a perfect heart and with a willing mind: for the LORD searcheth all

hearts, and understandeth all the imaginations of the thoughts: if thou _seek him_, he will be found of thee; but if thou forsake him, he will cast thee off for ever (1Chronicles 28:9).

And he went out to meet Asa, and said unto him, Hear ye me, Asa, and all Judah and Benjamin; The LORD _is_ with you, while ye be with him; and if ye _seek him_, he will be found of you; but if ye forsake him, he will forsake you (2Chronicles 15:2).

For I was ashamed to require of the king a band of soldiers and horsemen to help us against the enemy in the way: because we had spoken unto the king, saying, The hand of our God _is_ upon all them for good that _seek him_; but his power and his wrath _is_ against all them that forsake him (Ezra 8:22).

The meek shall eat and be satisfied: they shall praise the LORD that _seek him_: your heart shall live forever (Psalm 22:26).

Blessed _are_ they that keep his testimonies, _and that seek him_ with the whole heart (Psalm 119:2).

I will rise now, and go about the city in the streets, and in the broad ways I will _seek him_ whom my soul loveth: I sought him, but I found him not (Song of Solomon 3:2).

_seek him_ that maketh the seven stars and Orion, and turneth the shadow of death into the morning, and maketh the day dark with night: that calleth for the waters of the sea, and poureth them out upon the face of the earth: The LORD _is_ his name (Amos 5:8).

> But without faith *it is* impossible to please *him:* for
> he that cometh to God must believe that he is, and
> *that* he is a rewarder of them that diligently <u>seek him</u>
> (Hebrews 11:6).

So how does one seek God?

This is sort of a sanctification process, so I would like to share what I call a media fast, which is basically turning off: T.V.s, Radios, News Papers, Computers, Books, Magazines, and other forms of entertainment. If you have family, then ask them to respect you in this for a while, and give them a date when you will come off your fast. Next; spend all the time you would have spent doing those things praying and asking God to make Himself clear, read your bible, get one without study notes or helps, at this point you want your own revelations, not those that God gave to someone else. Find one that is easy to see and if you need a definition for a word then get a Strong's exhaustive Concordance with the Greek and Hebrew Lexicons. But for the most part just begin reading it from both Old and New Testaments a few chapters every day or whenever you have a moment. If you have questions, then ask God, and believe He will answer you. Most likely the answers will come through the scriptures you are reading.

If you feel the Spirit lead you to do something during this period, such as pray for someone, help someone, etc. then do it; remember obedience is better than sacrifice.

Unless you can take time off from work or daily routines, like supporting your family, feeding the kids, etc. you will need to talk to co-workers, your spouse, and other people in your life. This is fine but, try not to tell them what you are doing, and why you are doing it. Just like any fast this is between you and God, so don't let others talk you out of it. They may be well meaning, but they are not the

God you seek. Just be polite and tell them you are busy or have plans if they invite you to things. Remember, this fast want last for your whole life; it is a month or so that you are dedicating to the Lord, and the Lord knows you have certain things that demand your time.

During this Media Fast it is important that you also do not do any drugs, unless you need them for medical reasons, no drinking of anything fermented and only eat basic foods. If you decide to go on a food fast while going thru this you may; however, do not take unnecessary risks trying to garner God's favor. He loves you and the only thing that sets you apart from any other believer is your _faith_, your _tongue_ and your _obedience_, while fasting can have significant benefits it really only impresses God when you perform the fast He has chosen, so treat this Media Fast the same way.

> _Is_ not this the fast that I have chosen? to loose the bands of wickedness, to undo the heavy burdens, and to let the oppressed go free, and that ye break every yoke?
>
> _Is it_ not to deal thy bread to the hungry, and that thou bring the poor that are cast out to thy house? when thou seest the naked, that thou cover him; and that thou hide not thyself from thine own flesh?
>
> Then shall thy light break forth as the morning, and thine health shall spring forth speedily: and thy righteousness shall go before thee; the glory of the LORD shall be thy rereward. Then shalt thou call, and the LORD shall answer; thou shalt cry, and he shall say, Here I _am_. If thou take away from the midst of thee the yoke, the putting forth of the finger, and speaking vanity; And _if_ thou draw out thy soul to the hungry, and satisfy the afflicted soul; then shall thy light rise

in obscurity, and thy darkness *be* as the noonday: And the LORD shall guide thee continually, and satisfy thy soul in drought, and make fat thy bones: and thou shalt be like a watered garden, and like a spring of water, whose waters fail not *(Isaiah 58:6-11)*.

Talk to the Lord, let Him know exactly what you feel you need and what is going on with you. Do not try to hide anything because he already knows. The purpose for your speaking it out loud is so when he answers you will know it. God loves it when we speak words that he can fulfill. I know this sounds a lot like the blab it grab it stuff but this is not about being selfish it is about your need for God; to reach a new level in your walk with Him. At least that is what I felt when you posted this question.

~~~

# Chapter 10

## Science and The Bible

*"What is Science but what the Natural World has said to natural men? What is Revelation but what the Spiritual World has said to Spiritual men?" Henry Drummond*

*"Evolutionary Darwinists need to understand we are taking the dinosaurs back. This is a battle cry to recognize the science in the revealed truth of God." Ken Ham*

1. Does the Big Bang theory rule out Creation?
2. If the Earth was created 6000 years ago, did God create dinosaur fossils to test man's faith in the Bible?
3. Is it fair to say that a devout Christian, Jew, or Muslim does not believe in true randomness in the universe because he/she believes there is a god?
4. Is God separate from creation?

**Q.** Does the Big Bang theory rule out Creation?

**A.** The Genesis account of Creation does not tell the whole story of Creation. Let us see what it tells us about the very beginning.

> 1 In the beginning God created the heaven and the earth. 2 And the earth was without form, and void; and darkness was upon the face of the deep. And the Spirit of God moved upon the face of the waters. (Genesis 1:1-2)

However, in Proverbs the Lord says that God created the Earth with wisdom, and the constant companion of God's wisdom is peace. Proverbs chapter three shows that God's wisdom is life and peace.

> The LORD by wisdom hath founded the earth; by understanding hath he established the heavens (Proverbs 3:19).

We see that what God created, is not what He finds in Genesis 1:2 also look at what it says in the Gospel of John.

> 1 In the beginning was the Word, and the Word was with God, and the Word was God. 2 The same was in the beginning with God. 3 All things were made by him; and without him was not any thing made that was made. 4 In him was life; and the life was the light of men. 5 And the light shineth in darkness; and the darkness comprehended it not. (John 1:1-5)

When we look at evolution and what some scientist tell us it is in direct contradiction to Creation. The evolution theory describes a constant struggle for survival, yet the evidence of evolution is found not only in archeology but even in the daily dog eat dog world we live in. So as a Christian how, do I reconcile scientific discoveries with what is written in the Bible?

From what I see through all of this is that Genesis 1:1 is God's version of the "Big Bang" story. This very well could have started some 15 billion years ago. God is an eternal being and He does not measure time except to mark the end of violence and evil.

When you think about it, all science was in the "Big Bang." God designed the sciences as it suited Him; it is an attribute of wisdom. The laws of physics are the laws of God. While we humans see the Big Bang as a violent reaction, it was not violent to the Almighty who caused it to happen. We still think of the Sun as a very violent hostile environment but in the eyes of God and in His hearing the stars are symphonic and though we cannot understand it, the Bible says they sing praises to Him.

> When the morning stars sang together, and all the
> sons of God shouted for joy? (Job 38:7)

Now let look again at Genesis 1:2; the Earth is presented as "dark" and "void" but according to Proverbs God, "laid it with Wisdom and Peace." Wisdom is also translated as being a light source so it must mean that God created Earth in the Light and it was peaceful. In fact, a thorough study of scriptures will reveal that God designed Earth to be a perfect habitat for humanity. It was not until Satan rebelled that the Earth became "Dark" and "Void." This next question I go into quite a bit of detail of what happened between Genesis 1:1 and 1:2.

~~~

**Q.** If the Earth was created 6000 years ago, did God create dinosaur fossils to test man's faith in the Bible?

**A.** First, let me say that God does not dwell on the past though He does not forget it either. God is not concerned about the dinosaurs, as they are mostly an extinct kingdom, with only a few species remaining. They have little to do with man's relationship with God. The Bible's primary purpose is to show man's incapability to redeem himself, God's solution to ratify man, and bring us to something greater than when we were first created. Nevertheless, to provide some insight to this question I have outlined a possible chronology of events that are mentioned in scriptures, which might satisfy the question of dinosaurs and early human remains.

Please note I am not a scientist, but most scientists believe that a comet struck the earth and killed off the Dinosaurs. I believe that when Satan and a third of the angels were cast out of Heaven it caused a catastrophe. This is why the Lord had to speak for the light to shine upon the Earth and speak life back into the Earth in Genesis 1:2 again. What follows is what I believe are scriptures that are describing events that may have taken place in the gap from the beginning through Genesis 1:2.

### God's Existence before Creation

Time as we know it did not exist the term "beginning" or "Alpha" was some sort of eternity that we cannot truly comprehend.

> 1 In the beginning was the Word, and the Word was with God, and the Word was God. 2 The same was in the beginning with God (John 1:1-2).

### God Planned Creation

> The LORD by wisdom hath founded the earth; by understanding hath he established the heavens (Proverbs 3:19).

4 Where wast thou when I laid the foundations of the earth? declare, if thou hast understanding. 5 Who hath laid the measures thereof, if thou knowest? or who hath stretched the line upon it? 6 Whereupon are the foundations thereof fastened? or who laid the corner stone thereof; (Job 38:4-6).

### God Creates Heaven and Earth, and all things in them

This was probably billions of Earth's years ago as we account for time.

In the beginning God created the heaven and the earth (Genesis 1:1).

All things were made by him; and without him was not any thing made that was made (John 1:3).

### God creates Lucifer and anoints him

Lucifer was God's most beautiful creation at that time and was free to roam wherever he pleased.

13 Thou hast been in Eden the garden of God; every precious stone *was* thy covering, the sardius, topaz, and the diamond, the beryl, the onyx, and the jasper, the sapphire, the emerald, and the carbuncle, and gold: the workmanship of thy tabrets and of thy pipes was prepared in thee in the day that thou wast created. 14 Thou *art* the anointed cherub that covereth; and I have set thee *so:* thou wast upon the holy mountain of God; thou hast walked up and down in the midst of the stones of fire. 15 Thou *wast* perfect in thy ways from the day that thou wast created, till iniquity was found in thee (Ezekiel 28:13-15).

So why did Lucifer rebel?

## *God announces His plan to make man.*

> God said, Let us make man in our image, after our
> likeness: and let them have dominion over the fish
> of the sea, and over the fowl of the air, and over the
> cattle, and over all the earth, and over every creeping
> thing that creepeth upon the earth (Genesis 1:26).

I believe that statement caused Lucifer to become jealous and prideful
so he rebelled by starting the war in heaven. Once this war broke
out in heaven, evolution began on Earth. Not as a creative force of
God but as a desperate attempt for the life that existed to survive
and because of Lucifer's rebellion, the anointing that was on him to
praise God turned to self-praise or pride. This led to destruction and
caused all the violence in the Earth. Proverbs 16:18 says, "Pride *goeth*
before destruction, and an haughty spirit before a fall."

## *Lucifer rebels and starts a war*

It is also important to realize that Lucifer's plan was to take over
before God carried out the creation of man.

> 7 And there was war in heaven: Michael and his angels
> fought against the dragon; and the dragon fought and
> his angels, 8 And prevailed not; neither was their place
> found any more in heaven (Revelation 12:7-8).

## *Satan is placed on trial*

> 12 How art thou fallen from heaven, O Lucifer, son
> of the morning! *how* art thou cut down to the ground,
> which didst weaken the nations! 13 For thou hast

said in thine heart, I will ascend into heaven, I will exalt my throne above the stars of God: I will sit also upon the mount of the congregation, in the sides of the north: 14 I will ascend above the heights of the clouds; I will be like the most High (Isaiah 14:12-14).

16 By the multitude of thy merchandise they have filled the midst of thee with violence, and thou hast sinned: therefore I will cast thee as profane out of the mountain of God: and I will destroy thee, O covering cherub, from the midst of the stones of fire. 17 Thine heart was lifted up because of thy beauty, thou hast corrupted thy wisdom by reason of thy brightness: (Ezekiel 28:16-17).

### Satan is sentenced and falls to Earth as Lightening

For if God spared not the angels that sinned, but cast *them* down to hell, and delivered *them* into chains of darkness, to be reserved unto judgment; (2Peter 2:4).

And the great dragon was cast out, that old serpent, called the Devil, and Satan, which deceiveth the whole world: he was cast out into the earth, and his angels were cast out with him (Rev 12:9).

And he said unto them, I beheld Satan as lightning fall from heaven (Luke 10:18).

I think that when this happened it happened with such force that it caused the destruction of life and light on the Earth thus wiping out the Dinosaurs and all life on Earth. In Genesis 1:2 God has to restore the Earth and recreate life on it. He also divides time into days and seasons and so on so that He can eventually bring an end to all sin, sorrow and every evil that began long before man was formed from the dust of the Earth.

### God Renovates His Creation and Starts a New Clock

> And the earth was without form, and void; and darkness *was* upon the face of the deep. And the Spirit of God moved upon the face of the waters. And God said, Let there be light: and there was light (Genesis 1:2-3).

> In him *(Jesus)* was life; and the life was the light of men. And the light shineth in darkness; and the darkness comprehended it not (John 1:4-5).

> And God saw the light, that *it was* good: and God divided the light from the darkness. And God called the light Day, and the darkness he called Night. And the evening and the morning were the first day (Genesis 1:4-5).

Over the next five days, God renovates the mess caused by Satan's fall and creates life on Earth again. This time He does make man on the sixth day, and then He rests.

Genesis through Deuteronomy is chronologically correct but God did not give us all the details at the time these books were being written. Moreover, the Bible reveals very little about what human beings went through prior to the flood. It is likely that during this time while some humans prospered greatly they did so at the expense of others. As humankind began to spread across the Earth the struggle to survive and possibly inbreeding caused a sort of evolutionary process to take over which developed the skeletal remains of some early humans. These early societies failed which shows that evolution, as a process left to its own could not have been a logical step to modern man.

I hope that this will help some of you see that God is the creator and the Genesis account is true. While scientific evidence should not be ignored, it does not mean that the Scientist's theories are true or accurate. Even though my theory may not be any more accurate than the scientist's theories, it does allow us to see how these skeletal remains came into being without twisting the Scriptures at all.

~~~

**Q.** Is it fair to say that a devout Christian, Jew, or Muslim does not believe in true randomness in the universe because he/she believes there is a god?

While a person who does not, believes that true coincidences and randomness can occur because there is no grand designer.

**A.** I am a Christian, but I still believe there are some things that happen randomly, else, where is free will? I think God knows everything that will happen and can alter events at His leisure, if He were to choose. However, I do not think He micromanages everything. If that were true, then it would make Him responsible for evil and good. God is not at conflict with himself. He put humans in charge of everything on Earth and we are the ones responsible for evil, although we have help and influence from Satan.

Ultimately, God put the laws of the universe into effect and then made a covenant with creation not to interfere uninvited, except to remind humanity that He is there for us. To accomplish that He chose prophets to warn us of coming problems and offered solutions which require us to acknowledge Him and turn from our ways and follow His.

His final solution was to provide the ultimate sacrifice of himself by becoming human and as a human He lived, was tempted to do evil, suffered, and died, as all men do. During that time, He assumed no position of earthly authority, except that which was given to Him in the beginning. The miracles He displayed were also in Adam when God formed him from the earth and gave him authority over ALL the works of His hands.

As a believer I gave the Lord full reign over my life, put all my trust in Him trusting that He would do what is best not only for me, but would also work in the lives of those I love. What I have learned from this experience is that God still allows me to make mistakes. He has no desire to micromanage me, but He has a deep desire to teach me how to follow Him more closely. My life is a daily lesson, not always comfortable or easy, but in all things I have peace and He is always with me.

~~~

**Q.** Is God separate from creation?

If we define God as consciousness, awareness, intelligence, spirit, and love, how then can anything possibly be separate? If anything existed separate from or outside Consciousness, Consciousness could not be aware of it. Is it not that God is all and all is God, expressing? I suggest that all we experience as things and objects are illusion and that no boundaries can possibly exist.

**A.** It sounds like a nice idea, but God is more than just consciousness. God is in all, and through all working to save those that are lost and purge sin from those who trust in Him. Yet, there is a Glory of God, separate from parts of the creation that are knowable. This is not because God wanted it like that, but because if the fullness of the Glory of God were to approach the Earth, in its current state, it would have a similar affect as dragging Earth into the Sun.

God does not keep His distance because He does not care about us, rather because the sin in the Earth would destroy the Earth, if that much of the Glory came upon it. So instead, He calls people to Jesus who will wash away the sin and bring all who receive Him to a state than can withstand the presence of God.

> For this corruptible must put on incorruption, and this mortal must put on immortality. When this corruptible shall have put on incorruption, and this mortal shall have put on immortality, then shall be brought to pass the saying that is written, Death is swallowed up in victory. (1Corinthians 15:53-54)

~~~

# Chapter 11

# Sex, Marriage, and Relationships

*"A man doesn't own his marriage; he is only the steward of his wife's love." Ed Cole*

*"An individual Christian may see fit to give up all sorts of things for special reasons - marriage, or meat, or beer, or cinema; but the moment he starts saying the things are bad in themselves, or looking down his nose at other people who do use them, he has taken the wrong turning." C.S. Lewis*

1. When Christians Demand that People Have Sex Only Within Marriage, What Kind of Marriage Are They Talking About?
2. How do I change My Life?
3. If the only real marriage is an "ordained" marriage, does that mean Christians think non-Christians can't get married?
4. What are some tips for having a good marriage?

**Q.** When Christians Demand that People Have Sex Only Within Marriage, What Kind of Marriage Are They Talking About?

Do they mean biblical marriage (with Levitacal customs) Do they mean civil marriage (defined by congress instead of God.) Do they mean their own defined marriage? What sort of marriages count? If I cohabit with my GF and declare that marriage only between us will that count?

**A.** The only marriages that God recognizes or as Jesus put it; "What God has joined together let no man split apart," marriages are those that He actually does join. Humans in haste and driven by their own desires involve themselves in relationships and covenants with each other, without first consulting God.

The type of ceremony is not important, except that it be witnessed by other believers who are in good standing in the Church and the vows that are exchanged are Biblical. I highly recommend that Christian couples get premarital counseling, so they have a full understanding of what each expects of the other, and that the vows should never be considered a light thing.

Outside of that, I do not believe Christians should have the right to "Demand" their values on the general populace. True Biblical marriage is between Christ, a man and his wife. Marriages in the world are between societal acceptability, and the people involved. If the greater part of society holds Christian values, then there should be no law necessary to regulate marriage. Because the world largely ignores God, domestic laws have become necessary to protect the people who get themselves entangled in domestic marriages.

Personally, I believe Christians should not get involved in the political marriage debate. To me it shows a lack of faith and arrogance that we have authority to regulate the lives of non-believers. I like the idea of separation of Church and State and we should be grateful that we live in a nation that allows us to worship freely and allows us to choose our own spouse. If congress enacts a law of the land placing restrictions on, or defining a legal marriage then the Government has a foothold in to what should be a highly celebrated religious ceremony.

~~~

**Q.** How do I change My Life?

Nothing changes, but still I have to live a happy life. I want to live a satisfying, peaceful, bright, positive life. I want to live a happy life even when Life is giving me No reason to be happy.

I'm a 23 year old single person who doesn't wish to be married anytime soon. But deep down inside I do wish for a man to love me for who I am. Not just marry me because he has to get married. I want to fall in love and then get married. I have been friends with guys and have had excellent understanding with them but then I don't know what happens, they just leave. I have been praying since years to find the true love and done every possible thing to keep my relationships with guy friends good smooth so that they can go on to the next level (that doesn't include flirting or anything, I can't do that with "just good friends" until they fall in love with me). A couple DID fall in love with me and then God knows what happened, they stopped talking to me. I have never been clingy and any other possible thing that guys hate. After praying for so many years and my prayers not been answered, my belief that God listens to our prayers has almost shattered.

What should I do?

Also, meanwhile, when the life is not changing or giving me a reason to be happy, I still can't stay depressed all day long? 365 days a year? My university life, social life, family life, health, everything is just getting ruined. I stay depressed ALL THE TIME like literally ALL THE TIME and now I'm so sick of this constant condition that I'm in since years.

I like to be single but deep down inside now I really, really need someone and change my life (both, with and/or without him- until I find one i.e.) Please help!!

**A.** Wait... Stop... all those prayers did not go unnoticed and those fellows that said they loved you but then left... They were not the one for you. This situation is not so unusual and I am glad to be able to address this because you are experiencing something very common where faith is concerned.

You start out saying you do not want to get married anytime soon. Good... heck, I will say GREAT even. The friends that come and go, believe it or not are making you stronger for when the right one does come. It's probably not going to be an all peaches and cream, lovey dovey, whirlwindish relationship. Falling in love is painful; you think that person is everything your imagination creates, but the real person is just a person. When two people find each other and rush into a relationship blinded with high expectations, they learn all too soon that it is not at all what they expected.

Slow down, quit worrying about past relationships, and cultivate the one that is the most important. You know the relationship with the one who actually heard your prayers and caused all those fellows to move on. Get to know the One who knows you, your beginning, ending, and everything in-between. Get that relationship right, make it your primary relationship and He will make you into a wife who will hear great things about her husband, and He will give you a husband that will love you enough to put your needs ahead of his own.

You are only 23, still very young, be free and single, quit looking at "guy" friends as if they are supposed to be permanent fixtures in your life. If you are not in love with them then be happy that they have moved on. Rejoice if they find happiness. Your time will come, till then live free in Christ. I am always happy when I see someone else find love and happiness.

~~~

Q. If the only real marriage is an "ordained" marriage, does that mean Christians think non-Christians can't get married?

This was a thought I had a little while ago after reading quite a few quotes that were discussing Christians saying that legal marriages don't count as marriage because real marriage can only be ordained by God. But, if that's so, then does that mean Christians believe that people of other religions, or atheists for that matter, can't get married?

A. No, the Bible says that Christians are to live and abide by the laws of the land, except when those laws are an attempt to prevent us from following Gods laws for us. So if non-believers get married then their marriage is answerable to the laws that recognize it as a legal binding contract.

Jesus said concerning marriage, "That which God has joined together let no one separate" (Mark 10:9). But on the broader scale God will not join people as one flesh who are not saved. If a married person becomes Christian after they became married under the law of the land then the new Christian is not supposed to leave the unbelieving spouse but live the Christian life as a devoted spouse in hopes that the unbelieving will become a believer. But if the unbelieving spouse desires to divorce then the believing partner is free and may remarry if they find a suitable and willing person that is a Christian.

If a non-Christian couple that is married under the law of the land and they as a couple become Christians then God ordains the marriage as one flesh. If they choose they can go forward and have a Christian wedding ceremony and sometimes do. But there is no ordinance requiring them to do so in the Bible.

Marriage as defined in the Bible is between God, a Husband and a Wife. "For this cause shall a Man leave his Father's house and cleave unto his Wife and they shall no longer be two but become one flesh."

The Apostle Paul said, "The head of the husband is Christ and the head of the wife is the husband." Except Christ is the head of the marriage then God does not recognize it.

~~~

Q. What are some tips for having a good marriage?

A. I think one of the main things is that you have someone you can relate to as an equal.

Here are a few more things that might help in choosing a spouse.

1. Have similar interests and things you can do together
2. Have separate interests in things you can do apart.
3. Be willing to try new things.
4. Learn to dance with your partner.
5. Focus on each other's better qualities.
6. Reconcile differences quickly.
7. Never go to bed angry; especially at each other.

8. Always sleep in the same bed.
9. If you have to separate for a time, then call every day.
10. Never forget important dates.
11. Learn when the best time is to discuss the important things.
12. Learn to listen.

Remember you are both only Human and if you are both believers in Christ the number one thing is to put Christ first in each of your lives. Know this one thing, that a Christian marriage is a very holy union in the eyes of the Lord. If you put things in the right order Christ, marriage, kids, extended family, and jobs, then other things, you will also have the Lords favor, in all you do.

~~~